PIERRE TEILHARD DE CHARDIN

MODERN SPIRITUAL MASTERS
Robert Ellsberg, Series Editor

This series introduces the writing and vision of some of the great spiritual masters of the twentieth century. Along with selections from their writings, each volume includes a comprehensive introduction, presenting the author's life and writings in context and drawing attention to points of special relevance to contemporary spirituality.

Some of these authors found a wide audience in their lifetimes. In other cases recognition has come long after their deaths. Some are rooted in long-established traditions of spirituality. Others charted new, untested paths. In each case, however, the authors in this series have engaged in a spiritual journey shaped by the influences and concerns of our age. Such concerns include the challenges of modern science, religious pluralism, secularism, and the quest for social justice.

At the dawn of a new millennium this series commends these modern spiritual masters, along with the saints and witnesses of previous centuries, as guides and companions to a new generation of seekers.

Already published:
Dietrich Bonhoeffer (edited by Robert Coles)
Simone Weil (edited by Eric O. Springsted)
Henri Nouwen (edited by Robert A. Jonas)
Charles de Foucauld (edited by Robert Ellsberg)
Pierre Teilhard de Chardin (edited by Ursula King)

Forthcoming volumes include:
Karl Rahner
Oscar Romero
John Main
Flannery O'Connor
Brother Roger of Taizé

MODERN SPIRITUAL MASTERS SERIES

PIERRE TEILHARD DE CHARDIN

*Writings Selected
with an Introduction by*

URSULA KING

ORBIS BOOKS

Maryknoll, New York 10545

The Catholic Foreign Mission Society of America (Maryknoll) recruits and trains people for overseas missionary service. Through Orbis Books, Maryknoll aims to foster the international dialogue that is essential to mission. The books published, however, reflect the opinions of their authors and are not meant to represent the official position of the society. To obtain more information about Maryknoll or Orbis Books, please visit our website at http://www.maryknoll.org.

Library of Congress Cataloging-in-Publication Data
Teilhard de Chardin, Pierre.
    [Selections. English. 1999]
    Pierre Teilhard de Chardin : writings / selected with an introduction by Ursula King.
       p. cm. – (Modern spiritual masters series)
    ISBN 1-57075-248-6 (paper)
    1. Spiritual life – Catholic church. I. King, Ursula. II. Title. III. Series.
BX2350.2.T43213 1999
230'.2 – dc21
                                     98-52408

Contents

Sources

AE   *Activation of Energy* (London: Collins, 1970)

CE   *Christianity and Evolution* (London: Collins, and New York: Harcourt Brace Jovanovich, 1971)

HE   *Human Energy* (London: Collins, 1969)

HM   *Heart of Matter* (London: Collins, and New York: Harcourt Brace Jovanovich, 1978)

HU   *Hymn of the Universe* (New York: Harper & Row, 1965; London: Collins Fontana Books, 1970)

MD   *Le Milieu Divin: An Essay on the Interior Life* (London: Collins, and New York: Harper & Brothers, 1960)

PM   *The Phenomenon of Man* (London: Collins, and New York: Harper & Brothers, 1959)

SC   *Science and Christ* (London: Collins, and New York: Harper & Row, 1968)

TF   *Toward the Future* (London: Collins, and New York: Harcourt Brace Jovanovich, 1974)

WTW   *Writings in Time of War* (London: Collins, and New York: Harper & Row, 1968)

Permissions

Introduction

The Heart of
Teilhard de Chardin's Spirituality

At the Heart of Matter
A World-heart
The Heart of a God[1]

Teilhard de Chardin's name is widely known, but his works are
not easy to read nor easy to come by. This ardent Christian, an
internationally known scientist and prolific religious writer who
died in the 1950s, is one of the least understood and most mis-
quoted thinkers of the twentieth century. This may be partly due
to the fact that many readers are quickly put off by the difficulty
of his ideas, the unfamiliarity of his vocabulary, or the sheer
unavailability of his writings, now mostly out of print. Sometimes it is also said that his ideas are today generally accepted,
that they helped to shape the decrees of the Second Vatican
Council, and that there is no further need to study them. All
this can be vigorously debated and questioned on points of
detail. But even if Teilhard's synthesis of thought is more ger-
mane to the holistic, ecological, postmodern, and global ideas
of our time, his strong life- and earth-affirming spirituality is

---

1. P. Teilhard de Chardin, *The Heart of Matter* (London: Collins and New York:
Harcourt Brace Jovanovich, 1978): cited hereafter as HM.

only rarely fully grasped and comprehended. It is this spirituality above all, the strength and inspirational power of his spiritual vision, which deserves to be far better known because it can give so much to so many. It takes an effort to appreciate Teilhard de Chardin's deeply spiritual and dynamic vision of the world, alive with the energy and fire of the spirit. Yet one cannot truly understand his philosophy of life and worldview without knowing his profoundly personal and thoroughly Christian spirituality.

Most think of this Frenchman as a man of ideas and, what is more, ideas that are difficult to understand. But he was a man of extraordinary passion and sensitivity who combined a unity of heart and mind which is rare. His deepest desire was to see the essence of things, to find their heart and probe into the mystery of life, its origin and goal. In the rhythm of life and its evolution, at the center of the cosmos and the world, he saw a divine center, a living heart beating with the fiery energy of love and compassion. The heart is really a fleshly reality, but the image of this very flesh, this concentration of living, breathing matter, came to symbolize for Teilhard the very core of the spirit. The incarnation of God in the world was very real for him, tangible and concrete, understood and expressed with such a strong realism that it can be startling. It can shock us into an awareness whereby the narrow boundaries and constraints of common sense experience melt away in an intensity of perception and feeling that is linked to the palpable disclosure of the divine within and around us. Teilhard de Chardin is truly one of the least well known and most ignored Christian spiritual writers of the present age who, with a great visionary vigor, foresaw many of the material and spiritual issues that have to be addressed in the new twenty-first century.

His entire outlook on life was a profoundly mystical way of seeing the world, but his mysticism was firmly grounded in contemporary scientific research, which has so hugely expanded the frontiers of human knowledge and self-understanding. For

Teilhard, the mystic seer and believer, this immense research effort of humanity and the advances of contemporary science, notwithstanding their negative side effects and the new ethical problems they create, ultimately lead to the adoration and worship of something greater than ourselves, to the celebration of and surrender to divinity, to a heart and soul of the world.

Teilhard's incarnate spirituality of divinized matter and flesh, of the sacramental offering up of the whole world with all its toil and pain to God, is the very basis for holding together all the elements of his worldview, so that there exists a mutual interdependence between his spirituality and his approach to life in the universe. His universal, dynamic vision of the world, and of human beings in it, draws out the best of Christianity. It also creatively welds together science, religion, and mysticism in one unifying synthesis. It is a deeply sacramental vision suffused with great reverence and love for life. Many pages of his writings sound abstract and distant, even cold at times, but in his more personal essays, diaries, and letters we find the voice of a passionate human being in search of and in communion with God, a voice that celebrates the wonders of creation and speaks with lyrical fervor of adoration and mystical union with God through being immersed in and part of the great stream of becoming in the universe. He was a man who possessed an extraordinary power of words and a great sensibility, an acuity of perception, an intensity of seeing and feeling, a man always in need of touching the myriad forms of life. All the senses come into play in his writing, and the words he uttered can touch us in turn, seize our heart, inspire our imagination, and nurture our inner growth.

Teilhard wanted above all to communicate his vision to others; he wanted to make other people *see* and *feel* about God and the world in a way similar to what he had so deeply experienced and been moved by. Over the years he made several attempts to describe and sum up this vision in succinct essays with such titles as "My Universe,"[2] "How I Believe,"[3] and "My Fundamental Vision."[4] In one of them he wrote, "It has been my destiny to stand at a privileged crossroads in the world; there, in my twofold character of priest and scientist, I have felt passing through me, in particularly exhilarating and varied conditions, the double stream of human and divine forces. In this favored position on the frontier of two worlds I have found outstanding friends to help me develop my thought, and long periods of leisure in which to mature it and to stabilize it. And because of that good fortune, I feel that I would be disloyal to life, disloyal, too, to those who need my help, if I do not try to describe to them the features of the resplendent image that has been disclosed to me in the universe in the course of...years of reflections and experiences of all sorts."[5]

•

Who was this man? And what was his spiritual vision, his experience of God and the world in the first half of the twentieth century? And how far can this vision still help us in the twenty-first century?

Pierre Teilhard de Chardin was a French Jesuit, but also a distinguished scientist of human origins and geology who lived between 1881 and 1955. After his death he became well known as a writer on science and religion and on the place of Christianity in the modern world, reinterpreted in the light of evolution. Thus his writings represent in many ways a modern form of Christian apologetics and a reformulation of theological doctrines from an evolutionary perspective. The publication of his

---

2. In P. Teilhard de Chardin, *Science and Christ* (London: Collins and New York: Harper & Row, 1968), 37–85. Hereafter cited as SC, followed by the page numbers of the essay quoted from this work.

3. In P. Teilhard de Chardin, *Christianity and Evolution* (London: Collins and New York: Harcourt Brace Jovanovich, 1971), 96–132, cited hereafter as CE.

4. In P. Teilhard de Chardin, *Toward the Future* (London: Collins and New York: Harcourt Brace Jovanovich, 1974), 163–208, cited hereafter as TF.

5. "My Universe" in SC 38.

works raised much debate in the 1960s, whereas now they are relatively little known and almost unobtainable. Far less known than Teilhard's general worldview is his deep personal spirituality centered on the universal, cosmic Christ, the very heart of his faith. He was a fervent, thoroughly modern Christian mystic and a deeply caring pastor of souls who helped many of his friends and acquaintances in their understanding of the Christian faith, approached from an evolutionary perspective.

Born in the volcanic region of the Auvergne in central France, Teilhard belonged to an old aristocratic country family which, through his mother's line, was distantly related to Voltaire, the famous eighteenth-century French philosopher and rationalist. Teilhard possessed a sharp intellect and achieved the highest academic distinctions, but his deeply religious soul and sensibility had more in common with Pascal than with Voltaire, with that great seventeenth-century philosopher, scientist, and mystic who was another Auvergnat like Teilhard.

Brought up in a traditional Catholic milieu marked by a vibrant faith and strong religious devotions, Teilhard was endowed with a deeply pantheistic and mystical orientation, an innate tendency evident since his childhood and linked to some key experiences in his inner development and outer attitude to the world. His religious temperament was much shaped by the saintly figure of his mother who, from early on, taught him personal devotions to Mary and to the "sacred heart" of Jesus, and introduced him to the reading of the Christian mystics. His scientific interests in the development of the outer world, in geography, biology, and paleontology, by contrast, were initially stimulated by his father, who encouraged his children to collect fossils, stones, and other natural specimens. Teilhard always knew that it had been his father who had laid the foundations for his subsequent scientific studies and career.

Pierre was the fourth of eleven children, and like his brothers he was sent to a Jesuit boarding school, where he received an excellent scientific and literary education. While still at school, he felt called to become a Jesuit and entered the novitiate at the age of eighteen. As a young novice he undertook the traditional philosophical and theological studies customary in the Jesuit order, but when the French Jesuits were exiled from France, these had to be continued in the South of England, at Hastings in Sussex. It was there that he was ordained a priest in 1911.

But he did not neglect his scientific interests during his novice years and was out in the countryside collecting fossils whenever possible. For his teaching experience he was sent to a Jesuit school in Cairo, where he taught physics and chemistry from 1905 to 1908. The three years in Egypt were a deeply formative experience for him, for it was here that he first discovered his great attraction to the desert and the East. Years later this experience led him to write with great lyrical beauty about his decisive encounter with cosmic and mystical life which eventually culminated in such works as *The Mass on the World* (1923) and *The Divine Milieu* (1927).

It was in Hastings, during the early part of this century, that Teilhard discovered the meaning of evolution for the Christian faith after reading Bergson's influential book *Creative Evolution*. The theory of evolution made him see the natural and human world very differently; it made him realize that all becoming is immersed in an immense stream of evolutionary creation where every reality is animated by a "christic element." For Teilhard the heart of God is found at the heart of the world, and the living, natural world is shot through with the presence of the divine, with what he eventually was to call "the divine milieu." As he later wrote in his *Mass on the World*, the glorious vision of the world at dawn transfigured by the rising sun over the steppes of Asia, experienced during his first expedition to China, inspired him to make a deeply mystical and sacramental offering of the entire cosmos to the energy, fire, power, and presence of the divine spirit.

His deeply mystical experiences were followed by scientific studies in Paris, but these were soon interrupted by the First

World War. He decided not to serve as an officer but to remain in the ranks in order to be with the ordinary soldiers. He joined a North African regiment in which, as a noncombatant priest, he served as stretcher bearer and helped the dying and wounded at the front. After the war he was awarded several war decorations praising him for his dedicated service. The greatest praise, however, came from the North African Muslim soldiers who called him *Sidi Marabout,* an acknowledgment of his spiritual power as a man closely bound to God, a saint and ascetic protected from all injuries by divine grace.

It was at the front, in the mud and blood of the trenches, that he first discovered a rich, diverse "human milieu" not encountered before during his sheltered family life and religious upbringing. This formative experience led him later to speculate about the oneness of humanity, and it also shaped him into a writer. Almost daily encounters with death gave him an extraordinary sense of urgency to leave an "intellectual testament" in order to communicate his vision of the world which, with all its struggle and becoming, he saw as animated by and drawn up toward God. Thus he wrote a series of deeply stirring essays interspersed with prayers and powerful confessions of faith. Like all his religious works, these writings, entitled *Writings in Time of War,* were published only after his death.[6] It is here that we find the seeds of all his later ideas. It is quite extraordinary how in the midst of war Teilhard could commit to paper a great exuberance for life. He wrote with power and passion about the world reverberating with divine life, with the presence of God and the spirit. Seeing the unity of all things in Christ, he expressed the desire to be an "apostle" and "evangelist" of "Christ in the universe."[7]

---

6. See P. Teilhard de Chardin, *Writings in Time of War* (London: Collins, and New York: Harper & Row, 1968). Essays in this volume will be quoted by their title, for example "Cosmic Life," followed by the abbreviation WTW and the page numbers.

7. WTW 219.

After the war, he obtained his scientific doctorate and was appointed to a lectureship in geology at the Institut Catholique in Paris, where he could expound his ideas about evolution and the Christian faith. As these ideas soon led him into difficulties with the Catholic Church, which did not accept the teaching on evolution at that time, he was glad to take up an invitation in 1923 to join a fossil expedition to the Ordos desert in China. This important year in the Far East eventually led him to spend the greatest part of his scientific career in China (1926–46), regularly interspersed with expeditions and travels in both East and West. It was in China that he wrote most of his essays and books, especially *The Phenomenon of Man* (1938–40), which is his best known but probably most difficult work. This is not only because of the complexity of its ideas, but also because it is not always correctly translated into English. For example, its French title really means "The human phenomenon," for Teilhard's central question really was: what is the significance of the human being within the vast history of cosmic evolution, and what is the role of the spirit within the history of life?

After spending the Second World War in Peking, Teilhard returned to Paris in 1946, but as his situation was still difficult within the Roman Catholic Church, he decided to accept a research post in the United States. Lonely and marked by suffering, he spent the last four years of his life mostly in New York, where he died on Easter Sunday 1955, on the day of the great Christian feast of the resurrection which was so dear to him that he had expressed the wish to die at Easter. He is buried in a Jesuit cemetery in the Hudson valley, about an hour from New York.

•

Teilhard left a large corpus of religious and philosophical writings. It is not easy to know these in detail since they were published after his death over a long period of time, without any final editing by himself. His works are very rich and complex in content and are now virtually out of print in their English translations. Whereas his scientific papers appeared during his lifetime, his religious and philosophical works became widely known only after his death and took over twenty years to be published. Their publication raised a great deal of interest around the world. The reasons for the many misunderstandings about Teilhard are the great subtlety and extraordinary fertility of his ideas, but also the complexity and splendor of his vision, which bears powerful witness to the love, energy, and hope which the Christian faith can give to the modern world.

All his life Teilhard felt he had seen something new. Seeing God as Christ in all things brought together three dimensions: the cosmic, the human, the Christic. His vision was so intense that he likened it to fire, his experiences so strong that he noted early in his diary, "All that I shall ever write will only be a feeble part of what I feel." However abstract his essays became in later years, the metaphor of fire runs through them all. And so does the image of the heart, the living center of the human being which became for him a symbol for all centers, for the essence of reality itself. More concretely, the image of the heart stands for the vivid fire of divine love found in God's own heart, represented as the "sacred heart" of Jesus. From early on in his writings Teilhard spoke of the "heart of matter," the "heart of the world," the "heart of God." As a child and young man Teilhard had been taught the traditional Roman Catholic devotion to the "sacred heart" by his mother and the Jesuits. This devotion has medieval, pre-Reformation roots, but became particularly popular during the seventeenth century and was widely practiced in nineteenth-century France. As Teilhard has mentioned in his autobiographical essay "The Heart of Matter," he was never put off by some of the traditional sentimentality and narrowness of this devotion, but he reinterpreted it in his own original and universalizing way. Christ's heart became for him the powerful image of God's outpouring life and love pulsating through the whole of creation. From the smallness of the human heart it grew into a "furnace of fire" animating the whole world.

This spirituality of the heart is also closely connected with the Christian rite of the eucharist as an offering to and communion with God. The eucharistic elements — the bread and wine — is an offering of earthly realities to God which in turn becomes a sign of God's presence and love among human beings, an act of communion with and participation in the creative power of divine life. The center of the small host on the altar grows into an immense cosmic host, a sacramental offering of the whole world which includes all our achievements and sufferings, our joys and pains. In an act of communion, this all-inclusive offering can lead us to see a divine element at the heart of all our experiences, transforming each of them into an occasion for spiritual growth and renewal. Teilhard's spirituality is adumbrated in most of his writings, but it finds its most intense and powerful expression in the hymn-like prayer of *The Mass on the World* (1923),[8] the book *Le Milieu Divin: An Essay on the Interior Life* (1927),[9] also referred to as *The Divine Milieu*, and the two autobiographical essays written late in his life, "The Heart of Matter" (1950)[10] and "The Christic" (1955).[11]

What is at the heart of Teilhard's spirituality? Most central to it is a deep, intimate, and extraordinarily vibrant love of Christ — the human Jesus and the Christ of the cosmos, the ever greater, ever present Christ, the touch of whose hands we encounter deeply within all things. Teilhard's spirituality is animated by a fervent pan-Christic mysticism. The cosmic Christ, also called universal Christ, Super-Christ, and Christ-Omega, is the center of his worship and adoration, the core of his faith.

---

8. In P. Teilhard de Chardin, *Hymn of the Universe* (London: Collins Fontana Books, 1970), 13–35 (also New York: Harper & Row, 1965), hereafter cited as HU. The text is also found in a somewhat different translation in HM 119–34.

9. P. Teilhard de Chardin, *Le Milieu Divin: An Essay on the Interior Life* (London: Collins and New York: Harper & Brothers, 1960), hereafter cited as MD.

10. In HM 15–79.

11. In HM 80–102.

This is not only a "mysticism of knowing,"[12] but a mysticism of loving, of union and communion with all things, a fire and heart mysticism. All the images associated with fire — the glow, the spark, the flame, the blaze, incandescence and shining splendor — are used in his works again and again. They stand for the fire of love, the energy of the spirit, the breath and body of the living God, just as Moses met God in the fire of the burning bush, and Ezekiel was taken up in a chariot of fire to heaven, and as all-radiant light is associated with the New Testament event of Jesus' transfiguration.

Another important aspect of his cosmic-human-divine — or "cosmotheandric" — vision was "the feminine," a metaphor for "the unitive," the unifying power of love that brings together and unites, and thereby creates something new. Teilhard speaks of love like a thread running at the heart of the universe. Love is also the most powerful, specifically human energy that everybody needs just as much as light, oxygen, and vitamins. For Teilhard, to respond to the love of God, we must not ban other loves from our heart. We cannot grow and mature, reach plenitude of being, without the essential, emotional forces of love which we find in family, in friendship, in the love between two people. Teilhard was fortunate in his personal friendships and loves and had several close women friends whose formative influence he always acknowledged.

Teilhard's spirituality is deeply catholic in orientation, but in a universal rather than confessional sense. His thought has deep roots and resonances in the cosmic hymns of St. Paul, the logos theology of St. John, the writings of the Greek Fathers, especially Irenaeus and Origen, and the literature of Christian mystics through the ages which has always made extensive use of the images of light and fire to speak of God's presence.

12. See Thomas M. King's fine study, *Teilhard's Mysticism of Knowing* (New York: Seabury Press, 1981); also his general introduction *Teilhard de Chardin* in the series entitled Way of the Christian Mystics (Wilmington, Del.: Michael Glazier, 1988).

Teilhard lived a deeply personal and mystical spirituality in the midst of life, amid his actions and struggles, and he also wrote explicitly about spirituality in many of his writings. Three marks of his own spirituality may be specially noted. First, there is his harmonious integration of an extraordinarily active life of research, field work, and writing with contemplative and meditative modes of being and his pastoral concern and compassion for the spiritual well-being of others. This was the existential living out of what he described in *The Divine Milieu* as "the divinization of our activities and passivities." Teilhard was a great contemporary Christian mystic in the best tradition of Christian mysticism, but also a mystic in search of a new mystical way, a new spirituality open to the rhythm of the contemporary world and its ongoing development.

Second, his spirituality was expressed by the description of himself as a "wanderer between different worlds." He roved in mind and spirit among the worlds of the past, present, and future, but also among the worlds of science, religion, and mysticism. He also moved in body and mind among different continents, cultures, and peoples in West and East. These "wanderings" give his thought great concreteness and strength, for even his most abstract musings are always rooted in the experience of the real. Being a wanderer in and across different worlds is perhaps a vivid contemporary expression of the old Christian theme of being a pilgrim journeying through the world with and toward God. Teilhard undertook many journeys during his life, and wherever he went, he asked what spiritual gain and enrichment the very diverse experiences of his life, the joys and achievements as well as the suffering and pain, gave him, and what deeper spiritual meaning he could perceive through them. In all experiences of his inner and outer life he saw the hands of God shaping and guiding him.

Another, third aspect of Teilhard's spirituality was his profound loyalty, his fundamental and unshakable faithfulness to his vows as a priest, his permanent, unfailing commitment to his order and his Church in spite of many personal difficulties, doubts, and temptations. One can see in Teilhard a contemporary example of a "faithful servant of God" who overcame all trials in faith, hope, and love. He certainly experienced a great deal of anxiety, questioning, and hesitation, even shortly before his death, when he asked himself in his last essay, "The Christic," whether the wonderful diaphany of the divine at the heart of the universe, which transfigured everything for him, was perhaps no more than an illusion, a mirage of his own mind. Was his glorious vision of the universal, cosmic Christ perhaps an illusion after all? Might Christianity perhaps become extinguished in the world? After weighing up these large questions he eventually replied with a definite "no" and once again reaffirmed his belief in the overall coherence of the Christian faith and the contagious power of the love engendered by it. This strength of faith, this Christian fortitude to which Teilhard's life gives such eloquent witness, can be a tremendous source of strength and inspiration for others.

Teilhard's essay "My Fundamental Vision," written in 1948, is preceded by the words: "It seems to me that a whole life-time of continual hard work would be as nothing to me, if only I could, just for one moment, give a true picture of what I see."[13] More than anything else he ardently desired to communicate to others his profoundly spiritual worldview, his way of seeing, his particular perspective that integrated different insights and experiences. His essay "How I Believe" is preceded by the motto:

I believe that the universe is an evolution.
I believe that evolution proceeds toward spirit.
I believe that the spirit is fully realized in a form of personality.
I believe that the supremely personal is the universal Christ.[14]

---

13. TF 164.
14. CE 96.

These four sentences sum up his deepest convictions. The first relates to his scientific knowledge of the universe, the next two express a particular philosophy, and the last proclaims a religious position based on his Christian faith. Teilhard's brilliant gift for synthesis tried to connect and relate, not to fuse or identify, different aspects of human experience and exploration without keeping science, philosophy, religion, theology, and spirituality in separate and unconnected compartments.

•

As Teilhard's work is very extensive, many-sided, and complex, it is difficult to choose appropriate selections from it. Any specific choice can easily appear onesided and misleading. All the various aspects of his vision of the world and his Christian faith are so closely interwoven that no selective presentation can do it full justice. So many contrasting perspectives and approaches are possible. What I have chosen in this book is very much a personal interpretation which tries to give readers a taste of what is at the heart of Teilhard de Chardin's deeply lived spirituality.

I have grouped the selected texts under four headings: (1) Discovering the Divine in the Depths of Blazing Matter; (2) Living in the Divine Milieu; (3) Christ in All Things; (4) The Awakening and Growth of the Spirit in the World. Each section brings together different styles of writing — from the very experiential, personal, and devotional to the more reflective, analytical and descriptive. The various texts were produced at different moments of Teilhard's life and reflect different aspects of his experience. His religious writings were often addressed to quite different readers. Sometimes they were simply written for himself and his friends, but often they were addressed to those outside the Church, to sensitive, thoughtful, and searching contemporaries who were trying to make sense of modern life and find a spirituality that could give a deeper meaning to human existence. Other essays were specifically meant for Christians who have become doubtful and wavering, whereas others again are so deeply rooted within a Christian faith experience that they can be used as texts for prayer and meditation.[15]

Whenever I return to reading Teilhard's works, particularly his early seminal essays in the *Writings in Time of War*, I discover new insights and striking parallels to contemporary concerns. Teilhard sensed so vividly the great story of the universe, more fully revealed and known to us today. He perceived the earth as living planet and expressed his wonder at the beauty of the world around us, which he celebrated as a powerful revelation of the divine, the divine diaphany in and across all things. More recently, Brian Swimme has described the unfolding of these cosmic mysteries in an illuminating way in his book *The Hidden Heart of the Cosmos*.[16] Teilhard, the believer, knew and loved this heart at the center of the world as the heart of God. For Teilhard God was the most intimate presence whose insertion into the world through the incarnation meant that the divine runs through all of matter and life. God was also his closest friend and lover, his mother and father, a real person with whom he could speak and to whom he could communicate his innermost thoughts and doubts — someone he could love, embrace, and worship with all the powers of his heart.

The texts that follow are an invitation to meditate on Teilhard de Chardin's words, to be nurtured and strengthened by his vision, also perhaps to read more and discover further strands of his thought, so that readers may be inspired by other aspects of his life not described here.[17] More than anything else,

15. For another small selection of meditative passages see Blanche Gallagher, *Meditations with Teilhard de Chardin* (Santa Fe, N.M.: Bear & Company, 1988).

16. See Brian Swimme, *The Hidden Heart of the Cosmos: Humanity and the New Story* (Maryknoll, N.Y.: Orbis Books, 1996); also Brian Swimme and Thomas Berry, *The Universe Story: From the Primordial Flaring Forth to the Ecozoic Era: A Celebration of the Unfolding of the Cosmos* (San Francisco: HarperSanFrancisco, 1992).

17. For a fuller introduction to his life see my illustrated biography *Spirit of Fire: The Life and Vision of Teilhard de Chardin* (Maryknoll, N.Y.: Orbis Books, 1996). Further aspects of Teilhard's spirituality in the light of contemporary experience

the fire of Teilhard's words and vision may help to ignite a spark through their central spiritual insight about "living in the divine milieu." This is a particular way of seeing, of reflecting, and responding that holds the key to a secret that can transform every experience, every event, whether good or bad, into a significant encounter which reveals to us the breath and touch of the spirit, the ever loving heart of God. This particular way of seeing is also a spiritual discipline, a technique even, which can be learned and practiced. Its potential for transforming human life into greater growth and wholeness, into a sense of plenitude and an experience of communion, is immense. Understood in this way, the heart of Teilhard de Chardin's spirituality is truly linked to the transfiguration of ordinary life into an ardent adventure of the spirit.[18]

---

are discussed in my Bampton Lectures published as *Christ in All Things: Exploring Spirituality with Teilhard de Chardin* (Maryknoll, N.Y.: Orbis Books, and London: SCM Press, 1997). See also my earlier book *The Spirit of One Earth: Reflections on Teilhard de Chardin and Global Spirituality* (New York: Paragon House, 1989).

18. The selected texts have been taken from Teilhard de Chardin's collection of writings mentioned in the previous notes: *Writings in Time of War* (WTW), *Heart of Matter* (HM), *Le Milieu Divin* (MD), *Hymn of the Universe* (HU), *Science and Christ* (SC), *Christianity and Evolution* (CE), *Toward the Future* (TF). In addition I also have used texts from P. Teilhard de Chardin, *Activation of Energy* (London: Collins, 1970; cited as AE); *Human Energy* (London: Collins, 1969; cited as HE); and *The Phenomenon of Man* (London: Collins and New York: Harper & Brothers, 1959; cited as PM). As Teilhard's works were written before the days of inclusive language, he often used the word "l'homme," translated as "man" in English, when he speaks inclusively about human beings of both sexes. I have made alterations in the English translations to indicate this inclusiveness, but as not all texts lend themselves easily to such changes, the nouns "man" and "mankind" have sometimes been retained, but are always intended to have an inclusive meaning. All the passages selected for this anthology have been edited. In some cases this includes substantial cuts or an occasional word or sentence based on my own translation from the French original.

PIERRE
TEILHARD
DE CHARDIN

Chapter 1

Discovering the Divine
in the Depths of Blazing Matter

To understand the world knowledge is not enough; you must see it, touch it, live in its presence and drink the vital heat of existence in the very heart of reality.

— HM 71

The concrete tangibility of the earth, the fragility of the living world, the haunting beauty of nature — all these were for Teilhard potentially a means for divine disclosure. The human experience of the senses — of seeing, touching, and feeling — could reveal a path leading to the "heart of reality," to God. Teilhard possessed an extraordinary sense of physical concreteness, of the strength and revelatory power of all created things in this world. He also felt a great yearning for a deeper unity of all things, with all their diversity ultimately held together by God.

He was always fully aware how much he had been blessed by certain innate tendencies to seek what he called the heart of God at the heart of the world. Both science and religion helped him in this and, in their combined effect, made him see things differently. To see more and to feel more means to be more, to live a fuller, richer life, a life of plenitude and wholeness. "To see or to perish is the very condition laid upon everything that makes up the universe, by reason of the mysterious gift

of existence," he wrote in the foreword of his book The Phenomenon of Man *(PM 31). Teilhard's particular way of seeing
everything in an interconnected, holistic, all-embracing, unifying vision provided him with deep mystical insight and wisdom.
He wished above all to communicate his vision of the splendor
of the spirit and of divine presence to his fellow human beings.*

*To discover the elements of this deeply spiritual vision we
need to retrace Teilhard's inner development, expressed in his
spiritual autobiography "The Heart of Matter" written in 1950,
but also lyrically described in his early essays written in the
trenches of the First World War. His particular way of seeing consisted of three essential components which he called
"the cosmic, the human, and the Christic." The creative inter-
weaving of these three disclosed to him "the diaphany of the
divine at the heart of a glowing universe." The extracts in this
book relate to all three of these, but the texts selected in this first
section are particularly concerned with Teilhard's cosmic sense,
that is to say, with his experience of the earth and the universe.*

*From his childhood onward he had been aware of a strong
attraction to nature, of seeking and finding a sense of plenitude,
a sense of the whole in his discovery of the wonders of the earth.
He experienced this in the beauty of the natural environment
and seasons, in the richness of flora and fauna, in the rhythms
of living and dying and being born again. More abstractly, he
spoke of the appeal of matter, the communion with becoming, and his ever present longing to find the essence of matter,
its heart. His innate cosmic sense, a fundamentally pantheistic
inclination, awakened in him an awareness of the richness of
cosmic life, the immense abundance of the living biosphere surrounding the earth. Here his scientific studies of geology and
paleontology, but also of biology and physics, and his travels to
different continents greatly heightened his understanding of the
meaning of matter and life.*

*A key experience was the discovery of the meaning of
evolution, which led his creative mind in new directions. Under-*

standing the dynamics of evolution, the rhythm and meaning of change in myriad living forms, expanded his sense of plenitude and made him feel part of a much larger reality, a greater whole. Studying the without of things, their outer appearance and composition, he was led to discover their within, their heart and soul. The discovery of evolution — not as an outward mechanical process, but as a dynamic, living pattern in an evolutively unfolding universe — brought a tremendous breakthrough in his psychological, intellectual, and religious life. It tore apart the rigid divisions of the traditional dualism between matter and spirit by making him realize that these were not two separate things, but two aspects of one and the same reality. Not identical or fused together, but one leading to the other, blazing matter disclosing the fire of spirit. This gave him an immense sense of release, a great thrill and feeling of inner expansion. With extraordinary insight, sensitivity, and great lyrical beauty he praised the spiritual power of matter, flood of energy, and crucible of spirit.

Few contemporaries have so palpably experienced both the "temptation of matter" and the strength of communion with the earth, our great mother, whom Teilhard called by her Greek name "Gaia" in his essay "Cosmic Life." The ecstasy of the experience, but also the struggle and passivities endured in being part of a larger life, were expressed again and again by Teilhard. He spoke of hallowed matter and hallowed life, even of the holiness of evolution, but his Christian faith made him see the evolutionary stream of becoming as God's creative action of which we are an integral part. Therefore we can find and commune with God through the earth and through life. By trusting life, by fully participating in and cooperating with it, we contribute to the building up of the body of Christ. This is a deeply sacramental and incarnational vision of the entire universe and of the significance of the human being within it. It is also a deeply embodied spirituality with a profound reverence for all matter and life in their myriad forms.

A PARTICULAR WAY
OF SEEING EVERYTHING

I shall begin by describing the *fundamental tendency*, the natural cast, of my mind.... Then I shall describe how these innate dispositions gradually changed, for me, into a *particular way of seeing everything*, whether earthly or divine....

However far back I go into my memories (even before the age of ten) I can distinguish in myself the presence of a strictly dominating passion: the passion for the Absolute.

At that age, of course, I did not so describe the urgent concern I felt; but today I can put a name to it without any possible hesitation.

Ever since my childhood, the need to lay hold of "some Absolute" in everything was the axis of my inner life. I can remember very vividly that, for all my youthful pleasures, I was happy only *in terms* of a fundamental delight; and that consisted generally in the possession, or the thought of, some more precious, rarer, more consistent, more immutable object. At one time it would be a piece of metal; at another, I would take a leap to the other extreme and find satisfaction in the thought of God-the-Spirit (the Flesh of Our Lord seemed to me at that time to be something too fragile and too corruptible).

This may well seem an odd preoccupation. I can only repeat that it was a fact, and a *permanent* fact. I was never to be free from the irresistible (and at the same time vitalizing and soothing) need to find *unending* rest in Some Thing that was tangible and *definitive;* and I sought everywhere for this blissful object.

The story of my inner life is the story of this search, directed upon continually more universal and more perfect realities. Fundamentally, my underlying innate tendency ... has remained absolutely inflexible, ever since I have been aware of myself. It would serve no purpose here to give a detailed review of the various altars that I have successively raised to God in my heart. I shall only say that as I found every *individual* form of existence to be unstable and subject to decay, I extended the range of my search: to elementary matter, to currents of physical energy, to the totality of the universe — always, I must confess, with an instinctive predilection for matter (regarded as more absolute than the rest) that I corrected [in myself] only much later. . . .

Since my childhood, and in later days ever more fully and with a greater sense of conviction, I have always loved and sought to read the face of nature; but, even so, I can say that my approach has not been that of a "scientist" but that of a "devotee." It seems to me that every effort I have made, even when directed to a purely natural object, has always been a religious effort: substantially, it has been one single effort. At all times, and in all I have done, I am conscious that my aim has been to attain the Absolute. I would never, I believe, have had the courage to busy myself for the sake of any other end.

Science (which means all forms of human activity) and religion have always been for me one and the same thing; both have been, so far as I have been concerned, the pursuit of one and the same object.   — "My Universe" in HM 196–98

COSMIC SENSE —
A SENSE OF PLENITUDE

What I shall try to do in the pages printed here . . . is quite simply this: to show how, starting from the point at which a spark was first struck, a point that was built into me congenitally, the world gradually caught fire for me, burst into flames; how this happened all *during* my life, and *as a result of* my whole life, until it formed a great luminous mass, lit from within, that surrounded me.

Within every being and every event there was a progressive expansion of a mysterious inner clarity which transfigured them. But, what was more, there was a gradual variation of intensity and color that was related to the complex interplay of three universal components: the cosmic, the human, and the Christic — these (at least the first and the last) asserted themselves explicitly in me from the very first moments of my existence, but it has taken me more than sixty years of ardent effort to discover that they were no more than . . . approximate outlines of one and the same reality.

Crimson gleams of matter, gliding imperceptibly into the gold of spirit, ultimately to become transformed into the incandescence of a universe that is person — and through all this there blows, animating it and spreading over it a fragrant balm, a zephyr of union — and of the feminine.

The diaphany of the divine at the heart of a glowing universe, as I have experienced it through contact with the earth — the divine radiating from the depths of blazing matter. . . .

When I look for my starting point . . . I find that the first thing I have to do is to give a picture of . . . a particular psychological disposition . . . , and for want of a better name I shall call it the *sense of plenitude*. However far back I go into my childhood, nothing seems to me more characteristic of, or more familiar in, my interior economy than the appetite or irresistible demand for some "unique all-sufficing and necessary reality." To be completely at home and completely happy, there must be the knowledge that "Something, essential by nature" exists, to which everything else is no more than an accessory or perhaps an ornament. To know and endlessly to enjoy the awareness of this existence — I must indeed confess that if ever in past years I have been able to recognize my own self and follow my own development, it has been only by picking up this note or tint, or particular flower, which it is impossible (once one has experienced it) to confuse with any other spiritual emotion, whether joy in knowledge or discovery, joy in creation or in loving: and this not so much because it is different from all those emotions, but because it belongs to a higher order and contains them all.

The sense of plenitude, the sense of consummation and of completion: the "pleromic sense."

Throughout all that I shall call in turn and indifferently "sense of consistence," "cosmic sense," "sense of the earth," "sense of man," "Christic sense," everything that follows will be simply the story of a slow unfolding or evolving within me of this fundamental...element which takes on ever richer and purer forms....

I was certainly not more than six or seven years old when I began to feel myself drawn by matter — or, more correctly, by something which "shone" at the heart of matter. At the age when other children, I imagine, experience their first "feeling" for a person, or for art, or for religion, I was affectionate, good, and even pious: by that I mean that under the influence of my mother, I was devoted to the child Jesus....

In reality, however, my real "me" was elsewhere.

And to see that "me" properly, you would have had to watch me as — always in secrecy and silence — and without even any idea that there could be anything to say about it to anyone — I withdrew into the contemplation, the possession, into the so relished existence, of my "Iron God." *Iron*, mark you. I can still see, with remarkable sharpness, the succession of my "idols." In the country there was the lock-pin of a plough which I used to hide carefully in a corner of the yard. In town, there was the hexagonal head of a metal bolt which protruded above the level of the nursery floor, and which I had made my own private possession. Later, there were shell-splinters lovingly collected on a neighboring firing-range....I cannot help smiling, today, when these childish fancies come back to my mind; and yet I cannot but recognize that in this instinctive act which made me *worship,* in a real sense of the word, a fragment of metal, were contained and gathered an intensity of resonance and a whole stream of demands of which my entire spiritual life has been no more than their development.

The real point, however, is: Why *Iron?* and why, in particular, *one special* piece of iron? (It had to be as thick and massive as possible.) It can only have been because, so far as my childish experience went, nothing in the world was harder, heavier, tougher, more durable than this marvelous substance apprehended in its *fullest* possible form.... *Consistence:* that has undoubtedly been for me the fundamental attribute of Being. ...But until this very day...this primacy of the incorruptible, that is to say of the irreversible, has never ceased, and never will cease, indelibly to characterize my predilection for the necessary, the general, the "natural" — as opposed to the contingent, the particular, and the artificial....

Already this was the sense of plenitude, sharply individualized and already seeking for satisfaction in grasping a definite object in which the essence of things could be found *concentrated....*

It is a long way, however, from a piece of iron to Omega point.... And I was gradually to find, to my cost, to what a degree the consistence of which I then dreamed is an effect not of "substance" but of "convergence." I so well remember the pathetic despair of the child who one day realizes that Iron can become scratched and pitted — and can rust....

And then, to comfort myself, I looked for things that would take its place. Sometimes it would be a blue flame (at once so material, so impossible to grasp and so pure) flickering over the logs on the hearth; more often some more transparent or more finely colored stone: quartz or amethyst crystals and, best of all, glittering fragments of chalcedony such as I could pick up in the countryside. On those occasions it was essential, of course, that the cherished substance should be resistant, impervious to attack, and *hard!*

There was an imperceptible transition, but one which was later to have an immense importance for my spiritual evolution: for it was precisely through the gateway that the substitution of quartz for iron opened for my groping mind into the vast structures of the planet and of nature, that I began, without realizing it, truly to make my way into the world — until nothing could satisfy me that was not on the scale of the universal.

—HM 15–19

AWAKENING TO COSMIC LIFE

At the very beginning of my conscious life, in my efforts to attain and grasp the "solidity" to which my innate demand for plenitude impelled me, I tried above all to capture the essence of matter by looking for it in its most closely defined and concentrated and heaviest forms....

Then it was that my newly born attraction to the world of "rocks" began to produce the beginning of what was to be a permanent broadening of the foundations of my interior life.

Metal (such metal as I could find at the age of ten) tended to keep me attached to objects that were manufactured and so mere pieces. Mineral, on the other hand, set me on the road toward the "planetary." I woke up to the notion of "the stuff of things...."

Later, when I was studying geology, it might well have appeared that all I was doing was seriously and successfully to consider the chances of a career in science. In reality, however, during the whole of my life there was but one thing which would irresistibly bring me back to the study of the great eruptive masses and continental shelves: that was an insatiable desire to maintain contact (*a contact of communion*) with a sort of universal root or matrix of beings.

The truth is that even at the peak of my spiritual trajectory I was never to feel at home unless immersed in an ocean of matter....

So it was that the sense of consistence led to the awakening and expansion of a dominant and triumphant sense of the whole.

Over about twenty years of my life (from my leaving home

for boarding school until I began my theology at Hastings in Sussex) I can distinctly recognize in my memories the unbroken trail that marks this profound transformation. During this time, as I shall have to explain, the material object of my secret joy may well have varied with my age; moreover, there was an important break in my life: my entry into the Society of Jesus. But I now see that these different events were no more than minor superficial ripples on the fundamental current constituted by my awakening to the cosmic sense and the cosmic life. This was a powerful interior process, in the course of which I found that I was gradually being invaded, impregnated, and completely recast as the result of a sort of psychic metamorphosis into which, it would seen, there passed the brightest of the energies released by my arrival at puberty.

It would be difficult for me to work out again, or at least to explain in some detail, the complicated story in which, at that time of my life, the various threads were formed and began to be woven together into what was one day to become for me the fabric of the stuff of the universe....

First of all, of course, and forming the solid permanent core of the system, was my taste for geology: the primacy of material matter, "matter-matter," expressed in mineral and rock. I shall not re-analyze here...the central position invariably occupied by my passionate study of the science "of stones" throughout the whole of my spiritual embryogenesis.

Thus, between the ages of ten and thirty, at the heart of my absorbing interests and of my secret delights lay a continued and increased contact with the cosmic "in the solid state." Already, however in a semi-subordinate way, there was the newly emerged attraction toward vegetal and animal nature; and, deep below, there came one day, at the end of that period, my initiation into the less tangible — but how stimulating! — magnitudes disclosed by the investigations of physics. On either side of matter stood life and energy: the three columns that supported my interior visions and felicity.

Because of its apparent fragility...the living world greatly worried and disconcerted me as a child. On the one hand, when I thought of plants and animals, to the knowledge of which I was being initiated by my country life and my father's taste for natural history, I felt quite certainly drawn toward them by my constantly watchful "sense of plenitude." On the other hand, I had to justify to myself the interest aroused in me by objects so shockingly lacking in consistence and so perishable as a flower or an insect; and so I created for myself (or did I discover in my-self?) certain mysterious equivalent values whose psychological connection is not perhaps immediately obvious but which gave me just the same feeling of intense satisfaction. For the solid and incorruptible, I substituted the new and the rare. So far was this carried that for years, as I now smile to remember, the pur-suit in zoology and paleontology of "the new species" became one of the most important pivots around which my interior life revolved.... I retained my dominant sense of the universal, and even as I felt the glow of satisfaction as I put my hand upon a really treasured specimen, that sense enabled me to experience fundamentally only a delight in a more intimate contact...with what would later become for me "the biosphere." Secondly, there was the decisive effect made upon my mind, at the right moment, by my introduction to physics and physicists.

It was only for three years, in Jersey — and then for an-other three years in Cairo (1905–8) — that I studied and taught a pretty elementary physics: the pre-quanta, pre-relativity, pre-atomic-structure physics. This means that in this field I am, so far as technical knowledge goes, no more than an amateur — a layman. And yet I find it difficult to express how much I feel at home in precisely this world of electrons, nuclei, waves, and what a sense of plenitude and comfort it gives me. The consistent, the total, the unique, the essential of my childhood dreams — the vast cosmic realities (mass, permeability, radia-tion, curvatures, and so on) through which the stuff of things is disclosed to our experience in a form which is patient at the same time of being indefinitely reduced to elements and indefinitely expressed in geometrical terms — that mysterious gravity (whose secret I ingenuously promised myself, at the age of twenty-two, that I would one day dedicate myself to unlocking): it was surely there that I met those very "archetypes" which...I still use, even when I come to the Christic itself, when I try to express for my own satisfaction precisely what I mean.

Linking the animal world and the energy world there lies the common foundation of the rock world. From above this firmly cemented whole there flooded over me a first wave of the exotic, which sometimes affected me like a rich tapestry and sometimes seemed to bring me an invigorating draught of a new atmosphere. This was the East. I caught glimpses of it, and drank it in avidly, with no concern for its peoples and their history (which had not yet begun to interest me) but under the attraction of its light, its vegetation, its fauna, and its deserts. Such, when I was about twenty-eight years of age, was the somewhat muddled spiritual complex within which my passionate love of the universe was smoldering without as yet the power to burst into open flame.

The truth is that, without realizing it, I had at that time come to a standstill in my awakening to cosmic life, and I could not start again without the intervention of a new force or a new illumination. A dead end: or perhaps I should say a subtly hidden tendency to drift toward a lower form (the commonplace, facile form) of the pantheist spirit, the pantheism of effusion and dissolution.   —HM 20–24

DISCOVERY OF EVOLUTION

It was during the years when I was studying theology at Hastings (that is to say, immediately after I had experienced such sense of wonder in Egypt) that there gradually grew in me, as a *presence* much more than as an abstract notion, the consciousness of a deep-running, ontological, total current which embraced the whole universe in which I moved; and this consciousness continued to grow until it filled the whole horizon of my inner being.

What were the influences or what was the sudden jerk that caused this feeling to appear and drive its roots so deeply into me; how did the process develop and what were its stages?...I can remember very clearly the avidity with which, at that time, I read Bergson's *Creative Evolution*....I can now see quite clearly that the only effect that brilliant book had upon me was to provide fuel at just the right moment, and very briefly, for a fire that was already consuming my heart and mind. And that fire had been kindled, I imagine, simply by the coincidence in me of the three inflammable elements that had slowly piled up in the depths of my soul over a period of thirty years. These were the cult of matter, the cult of life, and the cult of energy. All three found a potential outlet and synthesis in a world which had suddenly acquired a new dimension and had thereby moved from the fragmented state of static cosmos to the organic state and dignity of a cosmogenesis.

At first, naturally enough, I was far from understanding and clearly appreciating the importance of the change I was undergoing. All that I can remember of those days (apart from that magic word "evolution," which haunted my thoughts like a tune: which was to me like an unsatisfied hunger, like a promise held out to me, like a summons to be answered) — all that I can remember is the extraordinary solidity and intensity I found then in the English countryside, particularly at sunset, when the Sussex woods were charged with all that "fossil" life which I was then hunting for, from cliff to quarry, in the Wealden clay. There were moments, indeed, when it seemed to me that a sort of universal being was about to take shape suddenly in nature before my very eyes. Already, however, I was no longer trying, as I had tried earlier, to apprehend and pin down the Ineffable Ambience by looking toward some "ultra-material." I was already turning my eyes toward some "ultra-living." I had experienced a complete reversal of my sense of plenitude, and since those days I have constantly searched and progressed in that new direction.

Let me draw attention a little more closely to this discovery and to the way in which I retraced my steps.

Until that time my education and my religion had always led me obediently to accept — without much reflection it is true — a fundamental heterogeneity between matter and spirit, between body and soul, between unconscious and conscious. These were to me two "substances" that differed in nature, two "species" of Being that were, in some incomprehensible way, associated in the living compound; and it was important, I was told, to maintain at all costs that the first of those two (my divine matter!) was no more than the humble servant of the second, if not, indeed, its enemy. Thus the second of the two (spirit) was by that very fact henceforth reduced for me to being no more than a shadow. In principle, it is true, I was compelled to venerate this shadow but, emotionally and intellectually speaking, I did not in fact have any live interest in it. You can well imagine, accordingly, how strong was my inner feeling of release and expansion when I took my first still hesitant steps into an "evolutive" universe and saw that the dualism in which I had hitherto been enclosed was disappearing like the mist before the rising sun. Matter and spirit: these were no longer two things, but two *states* or two aspects of one and the same cosmic stuff, according to whether it was looked at or carried further in the direction in which (as Bergson would have put it) it is becoming itself or in the direction in which it is disintegrating.

Those phrases, "to become itself" or "to disintegrate," were still, of course, terribly vague, and it would be several decades before they acquired a precise meaning in my mind; but in their own way they sufficed to confirm me permanently in an attitude or choice which was to govern the whole of my interior development and whose chief characteristics may be defined in these simple words: the primacy of spirit, or, which comes to the same thing, the primacy of the future.

Strictly speaking, no doubt, the mere fact of having seen the disappearance of the alleged barrier that separates the within of things from the without — or even of having realized that once we have knocked down that wall we find that an experientially and tangibly recognizable current runs from what is least conscious in nature to what is most conscious — that mere fact, I must admit, would not by itself suffice to establish beyond question an absolute superiority of the animate over the inanimate — of psyche over soma. Is there any reason, in fact, why the cosmos should not swing at will first to one pole and then to the other? Or, after a certain number of oscillations, why should it not finally and unalterably settle down in the matter position?...Surely these could be two of any number of evolutionary formulas?

These problems were inevitably to present themselves to me later on, and I can see that I solved them at least for my own personal needs....

It was to take me a whole lifetime to appreciate (and even then, alas, by no means completely) the unendingly constructive and at the same time revolutionary effect this transposition of value (this change in the very notion of spirit) produced upon my understanding, upon my prayer and action.

—HM 25–28

THE SPIRITUAL POWER OF MATTER

" ... Steep yourself in the sea of matter, bathe in its fiery waters, for it is the source of your life and your youthfulness.

"You thought you could do without it because the power of thought has been kindled in you? You hoped that the more thoroughly you rejected the tangible, the closer you would be to spirit: that you would be more divine if you lived in the world of pure thought, or at least more angelic if you fled the corporeal? Well, you were like to have perished of hunger.

"You must have oil for your limbs, blood for your veins, water for your soul, the world of reality for your intellect: do you not see that the very law of your own nature makes these a necessity for you? . . .

"Never say, then, as some say: 'The kingdom of matter is worn out, matter is dead': till the very end of time matter will always remain young, exuberant, sparkling, newborn for those who are willing.

"Never say, 'Matter is accursed, matter is evil': for there has come one who said, 'You will drink poisonous draughts and they shall not harm you,' and again, 'Life shall spring forth out of death,' and then finally, the words which spell my definitive liberation, 'This is my body.'

"Purity does not lie in separation from, but in a deeper penetration into the universe. It is to be found in the love of that unique boundless essence which penetrates the inmost depths of all things and there, from within those depths, deeper than the mortal zone where individuals and multitudes struggle, works upon them and molds them. Purity lies in a chaste contact with that which is 'the same in all.'

"Oh, the beauty of spirit as it rises up adorned with all the riches of the earth!

" . . . Bathe yourself in the ocean of matter; plunge into it where it is deepest and most violent; struggle in its currents and drink of its waters. For it cradled you long ago in your preconscious existence; and it is that ocean that will raise you up to God. . . . "

The man saw himself standing in the center of an immense cup, the rim of which was closing over him.

And then the frenzy of battle gave place in his heart to an irresistible longing to *submit:* and in a flash he discovered, everywhere present around him, *the one thing necessary.*

Once and for all he understood that, like the atom, man has no value save for that part of himself which passes into the universe. He recognized with absolute certainty the empty fragility of even the noblest theorizings as compared with the definitive plenitude of the smallest *fact* grasped in its total, concrete reality.

He saw before his eyes, revealed with pitiless clarity, the ridiculous pretentiousness of human claims to order the life of the world, to impose on the world the dogmas, the standards, the conventions of man.

He tasted, sickeningly, the triteness of men's joys and sorrows, the mean egoism of their pursuits, the insipidity of their passions, the attenuation of their powers to feel.

He felt pity for those who take fright at the span of a century or whose love is bounded by the frontiers of a nation.

So many things which once had distressed or revolted him — the speeches and pronouncements of the learned, their assertions and their prohibitions, their refusal to allow the universe to move — all seemed to him now merely ridiculous, nonexistent, compared with the majestic reality, the flood of energy, which now revealed itself to him: omnipresent, unalterable in its truth, relentless in its development, untouchable in its serenity, maternal and unfailing in its protectiveness....

Yes, of this he was certain: even for his brothers in God, better men than he, he would inevitably speak henceforth in an incomprehensible tongue, he whom the Lord had drawn to follow the road of fire. Even for those he loved the most his love would be henceforth a burden, for they would sense his compulsion to be forever seeking *something else behind them.*

Because matter, throwing off its veil of restless movement and multiplicity, had revealed to him its glorious unity, chaos now divided him from other men. Because it had forever withdrawn his heart from all that is merely local or individual, all that is fragmentary, henceforth for him it alone in its totality would be his father and mother, his family, his race, his unique, consuming passion.

And not a soul in the world could do anything to change this.

Turning his eyes resolutely away from what was receding from him, he surrendered himself, in superabounding faith, to the wind which was sweeping the universe onward.

And now in the heart of the whirling cloud a light was growing, a light in which there was the tenderness and the mobility of a human glance; and from it there spread a warmth which was not now like the harsh heat radiating from a furnace but like the opulent warmth which emanates from a human body. What had been a blind and feral immensity was now becoming expressive and personal; and its hitherto amorphous expanses were being molded into features of an ineffable face.

A Being was taking form in the totality of space; a Being with the attractive power of a soul, palpable like a body, vast as the sky; a Being which mingled with things yet remained distinct from them; a Being of a higher order than the substance of things with which it was adorned, yet taking shape within them.

The rising Sun was being born in the heart of the world.

God was shining forth from the summit of that world of matter whose waves were carrying up to him the world of spirit.

The man fell to his knees in the fiery chariot which was bearing him away.

And he spoke these words:

HYMN TO MATTER

"Blessed be you, harsh matter, barren soil, stubborn rock: you who yield only to violence, you who force us to work if we would eat.

"Blessed be you, perilous matter, violent sea, untamable passion: you who unless we fetter you will devour us.

"Blessed be you, mighty matter, irresistible march of evolution, reality ever newborn; you who, by constantly shattering our mental categories, force us to go ever further and further in our pursuit of the truth.

"Blessed be you, universal matter, immeasurable time, boundless ether, triple abyss of stars and atoms and generations: you who by overflowing and dissolving our narrow standards of measurement reveal to us the dimensions of God.

"Blessed be you, impenetrable matter: you who, interposed between our minds and the world of essences, cause us to languish with the desire to pierce through the seamless veil of phenomena.

"Blessed be you, mortal matter: you who one day will undergo the process of dissolution within us and will thereby take us forcibly into the very heart of that which exists.

"Without you, without your onslaughts, without your uprooting of us, we should remain all our lives inert, stagnant, puerile, ignorant both of ourselves and of God. You who batter us and then dress our wounds, you who resist us and yield to us, you who wreck and build, you who shackle and liberate, the sap of our souls, the hand of God, the flesh of Christ: it is you, matter, that I bless.

"I bless you, matter, and you I acclaim: not as the pontiffs of science or the moralizing preachers depict you, debased, disfigured — a mass of brute forces and base appetites — but as you reveal yourself to me today, *in your totality and your true nature*. . . .

"I acclaim you as the divine *milieu*, charged with creative power, as the ocean stirred by the Spirit, as the clay molded and infused with life by the incarnate Word. . . .

"Raise me up then, matter, to those heights, through struggle and separation and death; raise me up until, at long last, it becomes possible for me in perfect chastity to embrace the universe."   —HM 71–76

COMMUNION WITH THE EARTH,
THE GREAT MOTHER

When a human being has emerged into consciousness of the cosmos, and has deliberately flung himself into it, his first impulse is *to allow himself to be rocked* like a child by the great mother in whose arms he has just woken. For some this attitude of surrender is a mere aesthetic emotion, for others it is a rule of practical life, a system of thought, or even a religion; but in it lies the common root of all non-Christian pantheisms.

The essential revelation of paganism is that everything in the universe is uniformly true and valuable: so much so that the fusion of the individual must be effected with all, *without distinction and without qualification.* Everything that is active, that moves or breathes, every physical, astral, or animate energy, every fragment of force, every spark of life, is equally sacred; for, in the humblest atom and the most brilliant star, in the lowest insect and the finest intelligence, there are the radiant smiles and thrill of the *same Absolute.* It is to this Absolute alone that we have to cling, giving ourselves to it directly and with a penetration that can see through even the most substantial determinations of the real, and that rejects them as superficial appearances....

What in fact characterizes pantheist and non-Christian views is that the fundamental equivalent they introduce between everything that exists is produced, at the expense of conscious and personal life, for the benefit of the rudimentary and diffuse modes of being found in the lower monads....

One day, I was looking out over the dreary expanse of the desert. As far as the eye could see, the purple steps of the uplands rose up in series, toward horizons of exotic wildness; again, as I watched the empty, bottomless ocean whose waves were ceaselessly moving in their "unnumbered laughter"; or, buried in a forest whose life-laden shadows seemed to seek to absorb me in their deep, warm folds — on such occasions, maybe, I have been possessed by a great yearning to go and find, far from men and far from toil the place where dwell the vast forces that cradle us and possess us, where my overtense activity might indefinitely become ever more relaxed.... And then all my sensibility became alert, as though at the approach of a god of easy-won happiness and intoxication; for there lay matter, and matter was calling me. To me in my turn, as to all the sons of man, it was speaking as every generation hears it speak; it was begging me to surrender myself unreservedly to it, and to worship it.

And why, indeed, should I not worship it, the stable, the great, the rich, the mother, the divine? Is not matter, in its own way, eternal and immense? Is it not matter whose absence our imagination refuses to conceive, whether in the furthest limit of space or in the endless recesses of time? Is it not the one and only universal substance, the ethereal fluidity that all things share without either diminishing or fragmenting it? Is it not the absolutely fertile generatrix, the *Terra Mater,* that carries within her the seeds of all life and the sustenance of all joy? Is it not at once the common origin of beings and the only end we could dream of, the primordial and indestructible essence from which all emerges and into which all returns, the starting point of all growth and the limit of all disintegration? All the attributes that a philosophy of the spirit posits as lying outside the universe, do they not in fact lie at the opposite pole? Are they not realized and are they not to be attained in the depths of the world, in divine matter?...

In the exhilaration, then, of these first delights and this first encounter, I may well have believed in the glitter, the sweet scents, the boundless expanses, the bottomless depths, and surrendered myself to matter. I wished to see whether, as the vast hopes aroused in me by "awakening to the cosmos" suggested, I could arrive at the very heart of things; whether, by losing myself in the world's embrace, I could find its soul. Ardently and with no holding back, I made the experiment, unable to imagine that the true could fail to coincide with the enchantment of the senses and the alleviation of suffering. But I found that the more I allowed myself to drift closer to the center, ever more diffuse and dilated, of primordial consciousness, the more the light of life was dimmed in me.

In the first place, I felt that I was less a part of society; for matter is jealous and will allow the initiate of its mysteries no witness....

What happened, however, was this: by the inexorable logic that links the stages of our activity, a diminution of social contact led, in me, to a diminution of personality. The man who finds his neighbor too heavy a burden must inevitably be weary already of bearing the burden of his own self. Thus I found myself seeking to cut down the work that every living being must produce if he is to remain himself. I was glad to see my responsibilities reduced; I could feel my cult of passivity being extended to the very limit.... And thus it was that in one flash the bewitching voice that was drawing me far from the cities into the untrodden, silent spaces, came through to me. One day I understood the meaning of the words it spoke to me; they stirred the little-known depths of my being, holding out the promise of some great bliss-giving repose; and I knew what it meant when it whispered "Take the easier road...."

It was then that faith in life saved me.

Life! When trouble lies heaviest upon us, whither shall we turn, if not to the ultimate criterion, the supreme verdict, of life's success and the roads that lead to it? When every certainty is shaken and every utterance falters, when every principle appears doubtful, then there is only one ultimate belief on which we can base our rudderless interior life: the belief *that there is an absolute direction of growth,* to which both our duty and our happiness demand that we should conform; and that *life advances in that direction,* taking the most direct road. I have contemplated nature for so long, and have so loved her countenance, recognized unmistakably as hers, that I now have a deep conviction, dear to me, infinitely precious and unshakable, the humblest and yet the most fundamental in the whole structure of my convictions, that *life is never mistaken,* either about its road or its destination. No doubt, it does not define intellectually for us any God or any dogma; but it shows us by what road all those will come that are neither lies nor idols; it tells us toward what part of the horizon we must steer if we are to see the dawn light grow more intense. I believe this in virtue of all my experience and of all my thirst for greater happiness: there is indeed an *absolute* fuller-being and an *absolute* better-being, and they are rightly to be described as a progress in consciousness, in freedom, and in moral sense. Moreover, these higher degrees of being are to be attained by concentration, purification, and maximum effort....

The true summons of the cosmos is a call consciously to share in the great work that goes on within it; it is not by drifting down the current of things that we shall be united with their one, single, soul, but by fighting our way, with them, toward some goal still to come.

— "Cosmic Life" in WTW 28–32

IMMERSED IN GOD'S CREATIVE ACTION

"The world is still being created, and it is Christ who is reaching his fulfillment in it." When I heard and understood that saying, I looked around and I saw, as though in an ecstasy, that *through all nature I was immersed in God.* The whole inextricably tangled and compressive network of material interconnections, the whole *plexus* of fundamental currents once again confronted me, just as it did when first my eyes were opened; but now they were animated and transfigured, for their dominance, their charm, and their appeal, all beyond number or measure, appeared to me in a glow of illumination and I saw them hallowed and divinized in both their operation and their future. "God is everywhere," St. Angela of Foligno said, "God is everywhere...."

Every exhalation that passes through me, envelops me, or captivates me, emanates, without any doubt, from the heart of God; like a subtle and essential energy, it transmits the pulsations of God's will. Every encounter that brings me a caress, that spurs me on, that comes as a shock to me, that bruises or breaks me, is a contact with the hand of God, which assumes countless forms and yet always commands our worship. Every element of which I am made up is an overflow from God. When I surrender myself to the embrace of the visible and tangible universe, I am able to be in communion with the invisible that purifies, and to incorporate myself in the Spirit without blemish.

God is vibrant in the ether; and through the ether he makes his way into the very marrow of my material substance. Through him, all bodies come together, exert influence upon one another, and sustain one another in the unity of the all-embracing sphere, the confines of whose surface outrun our imagination.

God is at work within life. He helps it, raises it up, gives it the impulse that drives it along, the appetite that attracts it, the growth that transforms it. I can feel God, touch him, "live" him in the deep biological current that runs through my soul and carries it with it.

God shines through and is personified in humankind. It is he to whom I lend a hand in the person of my fellow man; it is his voice I hear when orders come to me from those who have authority over me — and again, as though in a further zone of matter, I meet and am subject to the dominating and penetrating contact of his hand at the higher level of collective and social energies.

The deeper I descend into myself, the more I find God at the heart of my being; the more I multiply the links that attach me to things, the more closely does he hold me — the God who pursues in me the task, as endless as the whole sum of centuries, of the incarnation of his Son.

Blessed passivities that intertwine through every fiber of my body and my soul; hallowed life, hallowed matter, through whom, at the same time as through grace, I am in communion with the genesis of Christ since, when I obediently lose myself in your vast folds, I am immersed in God's creative action, whose hand has never ceased, from the beginning of time, to mold the human clay that is destined to constitute the Body of his Son — to your sovereign power I swear allegiance; I surrender myself to you, I take you to myself, I give you my love. I am happy that Another should lead me and make me go whither my own will would not take me. I bless the vicissitudes, the good fortune, the misadventures of my career. I bless my own character, my virtues, my faults...my blemishes. I love my own self, in the form in which it was given to me and in the form in which my destiny molds me. What is more, I strive to guess and anticipate the lightest breezes that call to me, so that I may spread my sails more widely to them....

And in this first basic vision we begin to see how the kingdom of God and the cosmic love may be reconciled: the bosom of Mother Earth is in some way the bosom of God.

We are not, however, simply nurslings rocked and suckled by Mother Earth. Like children who have grown up, we must learn to walk by ourselves and give active help to the mother who bore us. If, then, we make up our minds to accept wholeheartedly the manifestations of the divine will registered in the laws of nature, our obedience must make us throw ourselves into positive effort, our cult of passivities must ultimately be transformed into a passion for work. What, we now see, we have to do is not simply to forward a human task but, in some way, to bring Christ to completion; we must, therefore, devote ourselves with still more ardor, even in the natural domain, to the cultivation of the world....

To establish the truth of this statement it would not, strictly speaking, be essential to define in what way the world's progress toward perfection, whether natural or achieved through human skill, can truly contribute to the plenitude of Christ. Since immanent progress is the natural soul of the cosmos, and since the cosmos is centered on Christ, it must be accepted as proved that, in one way or another, collaboration with the development of the cosmos holds an essential and prime position among the duties of the Christian. It is in one single movement that nature grows in beauty and the body of Christ reaches its full development....

Natural evolution...seems now to be fully occupied with what concerns the soul. From being organic and predominantly determined it has become predominantly psychological and conscious; but it is not dead, nor has its reach even been shortened.... Who knows *what astonishing species and natural gradations* of soul are even now being produced by the persevering effort of science, of moral and social systems — without which the beauty and perfection of the mystical body would never be realized?

Supposing we carry our human ambitions to their furthest limit: hitherto we have refused to admit that anything absolute in the cosmic stock, from which mature souls are detached, will endure. What pusillanimity of concept made us do so, what right had we to? In its dogmas and sacraments, the whole economy of the Church teaches us respect for matter and insists on its value. Christ wished to assume, and had to assume, a real flesh. He sanctifies human flesh by a specific contact. He makes ready, physically, its resurrection. In the Christian concept, then, *matter retains its cosmic role as the basis, lower in order but primordial and essential, of union;* and, by assimilation to the body of Christ, some part of matter is destined to pass into the foundations and walls of the heavenly Jerusalem....

If *concern for progress* and the *cult of the earth* are given as their final end the fulfillment of Christ, why should not they be transformed into a *great virtue,* as yet unnamed, which would be *the widest form of the love of God, found and served in creation?*...

Let us pray:

Lord Jesus Christ, you truly contain within your gentleness, within your humanity, all the unyielding immensity and grandeur of the world. And it is because of this, it is because there exists in you this ineffable synthesis of what our human thought and experience would never have dared join together in order to adore them — element and totality, the one and the many, mind and matter, the infinite and the personal; it is because of the indefinable contours which this complexity gives to your appearance and to your activity, that my heart, enamored of cosmic reality, gives itself passionately to you.

I love you, Lord Jesus, because of the multitude who shelter within you and whom, if one clings closely to you, one can hear with all the other beings murmuring, praying, weeping....

I love you as the source, the activating and life-giving ambience, the term and consummation, of the world, even of the natural world, and of its process of becoming.

You the Center at which all things meet and which stretches out over all things so as to draw them back into itself: I love you for the extensions of your body and soul to the farthest corners of creation through grace, through life, and through matter.

Lord Jesus, you who are as gentle as the human heart, as fiery as the forces of nature, as intimate as life itself, you in whom I can melt away and with whom I must have mastery and freedom: I love you as a world, as *this* world which has captivated my heart; and it is you, I now realize, that my brother men, even those who do not believe, sense and see through the magic immensities of the cosmos.

Lord Jesus, you are the center toward which all things are moving: if it be possible, make a place for us all in the company of those elect and holy ones whom your loving care has liberated one by one from the chaos of our present existence and who now are being slowly incorporated into you in the unity of the new earth.

To live the cosmic life is to live dominated by the consciousness that one is an atom in the body of the mystical and cosmic Christ. The person who so lives dismisses as irrelevant a host of preoccupations that absorb the interest of other people. Such a person's life is open to larger horizons and such a person's heart is always more receptive.

There you have my intellectual testament.

       — "Cosmic Life" in WTW 60–62, 64–65, 69–70

Chapter 2

Living in the Divine Milieu

God is as pervasive and perceptible as the atmosphere in which we are bathed. He encompasses us on all sides, like the world itself. —MD 14

Teilhard's ardent spirituality was nourished by his Christian faith, but also deeply embedded in a unifying worldview, a unique synthesis which brought together elements of science, philosophy, religion, and spirituality. He always looked for a pattern in the development of things and asked above all about the significance of the human being in the vast universe. His search for overall oneness, for the unification of all things, made him see the unity of matter and spirit. Thus the universal stream of becoming, which is evolution, was understood as a process of progressive spiritualization through increasing union.

Together with his cosmic sense, present within him since childhood as an increasing disclosure of the divine suffused in the world around him, he discovered a sense of the human and of the specific nature of human reflection. Besides the biosphere, he also spoke of the "noosphere," by which he meant a layer of thinking and interaction between people around the globe. This great revelation of the oneness of humanity around the earth had dawned upon him first at the front, during the First World War when he silently contemplated the fullness of the moon suspended above the earth. He then realized that, in spite of the turmoil of war and dissension, humankind is drawing more closely together to form a greater unity. To explain how this is going to happen, he developed his theory of "creative union," which tries to set out how the many can become one, not through fusion and loss of identity, but through a higher form of union which differentiates between the individual elements while bringing them together in a deeper union. This is a new, complex synthesis of a higher order which produces something new, and whose ultimate outcome or spiritual summit Teilhard called "Omega."

Spirit and matter are not identical or fused, but they are intricately and mysteriously interrelated. They are not two separate things or natures, as those who insist on strict divisions maintain, but they are for Teilhard two directions within the evolution of the world. Spiritualization occurs through union, and all consistence comes from spirit. Even the simplest things in the universe possess the rudiments of immanence, a spark of the spirit.

Teilhard wrote extensively on the significance of the human phenomenon, not only in his famous book The Phenomenon of Man *(1938–40), but also in two earlier essays of 1928 and 1930. These bear the same title as the book, and it is from the first essay that an extract has been chosen here to express the importance of the human being in the development of the universe. Already in this early piece Teilhard was concerned with the problem of human action and with the question of what energy resources are needed for maintaining and developing the dynamics of the noosphere. His chief concern was to point out the need to feed the zest or ardor for life and to develop a human energetics to do so.*

The spiritual practice appropriate to such concerns is fully described in Teilhard's book The Divine Milieu *(1927), written "For those who love the world," as its dedication says. It troubled Teilhard immensely that while science has revealed the immensity and unity of the world all around us, the implica-*

tions of our tremendously changed worldview have not yet been fully incorporated into theology and religious practice. More theologians may be concerned with the relationship between science and religion today than was the case during Teilhard's own lifetime, but there is no one else who has ever so radically thought through the ramifications of the contemporary scientific and ecological worldview for the practice of spirituality as he did. Teilhard wrote The Divine Milieu *as someone "who believes himself to feel deeply in tune with his own times," and someone who sought "to teach how to see God everywhere, to see him in all that is most hidden, most solid, and most ultimate in the world" (MD 15). He conceived of his book as an essay "on life or on inward vision," not specifically addressed to Christians but to those who primarily listen "to the voices of the earth," and "to the waverers" both inside and outside the Church (MD 11).*

"Divine milieu" is an expression which tries to capture the meaning of two different experiences. On the one hand it refers to an entire environment, like the atmosphere which surrounds us and the air we breathe. On the other hand it also means at the same time a central point, a center where all realities come together, meet, and converge. The divine presence in the world is this mysterious "milieu" radiating throughout all levels of the universe, through matter, life, and human experience. We are immersed in this milieu, we are bathed in it. It can invade our whole being and transform us, if we but let it. Teilhard called it also a "mystical milieu," a "divine ocean" in which our soul may be swept away and divinized. All realities, all experiences, all our activities, all our joys and suffering, have this potential for divinization, for being set on fire through the outpouring of divine love.

Elsewhere Teilhard refers to the image of "the burning bush," drawn from the Hebrew Bible, to convey something of this great fire of the spirit pervading the world. In The Divine Milieu *another image from the same source is also called upon, the struggle of Jacob wrestling with the angel. This is a metaphor for the struggle of human life, its advances and diminishments. For Teilhard the essence of spiritual practice is to establish ourselves in the divine milieu, to live and die in it, to become part of it. Thus we find plenitude, fullness of being, which leads us to the Omega point, identified with the incarnate flesh of Christ in matter.*

To be surrounded by the divine milieu like an atmosphere that we breathe, like an ocean that we are immersed in, is celebrated in the hymn-like offering of all human experiences, of toil and pain, and of the earth itself, in The Mass on the World. *To say "a Mass on all things" had been Teilhard's prayerful meditation practice in the trenches when he was unable to celebrate the customary Christian liturgy of the Mass, offering bread and wine on an altar in a church. He first recorded this practice in his essay "The Priest" (1918), from which the section on "Communion" is reprinted in the Postscript at the end of this book. In 1923, when he was on an expedition on the Yellow River in China, he was in a similar situation in that he could not say Mass. Instead, he symbolically offered the entire cosmos up to God and left us his great visionary and inspirational piece* The Mass on the World, *which celebrates the magnificent grandeur, power, and beauty of the divine milieu among us, the milieu which Teilhard loved so intensely, the ambience in which he lived, worked, and died.*

THE HUMAN BEING
WITHIN THE UNIVERSE

Today man (or, to speak more correctly, the *human*) forms the pivot upon which the whole structure of my interior universe rests, around which its links are formed and it coheres and moves. Yet the human was far from occupying this cardinal position in my picture of the world immediately and without resistance. . . .

The more the primacy of the cosmic asserted itself in my mind, and the more I felt its appeal, the more, by contrast, did the human confuse and disturb me by the preponderance assumed at its level by "the individual," "the accidental," "the artificial. . . . " In man, did not the plural inevitably, and disastrously, break through and tear apart the universal and the total? . . . It was not merely that the trees prevented me from *seeing* the wood — the wood hardly even seemed to *subsist* behind them. . . .

It was only, if I am not mistaken, in an article on man, written about 1927 (that is, after my first visit to China), that I first allowed myself — on the model of Suess's biosphere — to use the term "noosphere" for the earth's thinking envelope. But although the word appeared in my writings at that comparatively late date, it was ten years earlier that the vision itself had germinated in my mind through prolonged contact with the huge masses of humankind that were then facing one another in the trenches of France, from the Yser to Verdun.

The atmosphere of "the front": it was, I am quite sure, from having plunged into that atmosphere — from having been soaked in it for months and months on end — and precisely where it was at its most dense and heavily charged, that I ceased to notice any break (if not any difference) between "physical" and "moral," between "natural" and "artificial." The "human-million," with its psychic temperature and its internal energy, became for me a magnitude as evolutively, and therefore as biologically, real as a giant molecule of protein. I was later to be astonished on many occasions to find in my own circle that those who could not agree with me suffered from a complete inability to understand that precisely because the individual human being represents a *corpuscular magnitude* he *must* be subject to the same development as every other species of corpuscles in the world: that means that he *must* coalesce into physical relationships and groupings that belong to a higher order than his.... This gift or faculty of *perceiving* without actually *seeing*, the reality and organicity of collective magnitudes is still comparatively rare: but I have no doubt at all that it was the experience of the war that brought me this awareness and developed it in me *as a sixth sense.*

Once I had acquired this complementary sense, what emerged into my field of perception was literally a new universe. By the side of (or above) the universe of large masses, I saw the universe of large complexes. Looking at the earth, my first instinct would originally have been to give particular consideration to what was most central and heaviest (the barysphere, we might say). As things were, my attention and my interest (still guided by the same fundamental need for solidity and incorruptibility) were gradually and almost imperceptibly climbing up from the extremely simple central core of the planet to its ridiculously thin, but dauntingly active and complex, peripheral layers. It was not merely that I found no difficulty in apprehending, more or less intuitively, the organic unity of the living membrane which is stretched like a film over the lustrous surface of the star which holds us. There was something more: around this sentient protoplasmic layer, an ultimate envelope was beginning to become apparent to me, taking on its own individuality and gradually detaching itself like a luminous *aura.* This envelope was not only conscious but thinking, and from the time when I first became aware of it, it was always there that I found concentrated, in an ever more dazzling and consistent form, the essence or rather the very soul of the earth....

The oneness of *unicity,* of man stretched like a veil over the confused multitude of living beings: this astounding singleness in cohesion was in itself sufficient to catch and fascinate my passion for the cosmic-apprehended-in-its-extreme-forms. Nevertheless it was only a first approximation in the story of my discovery of the human — or (which may seem a better way of expressing it) it was a first breakthrough which illuminated the very nature of the stuff of the noosphere considered from the point of view of its underlying structure.

Deep down, there is in the substance of the cosmos a primordial disposition, *sui generis,* for self-arrangement and self-involution.

As we proceed, we find that a certain degree of vitalized matter's physico-chemical arrangement brings a critical point "of reflection," which releases the whole train of the specific properties of the human.

Finally, as a result of reflection, we find a demand for, and a germinating principle of, complete and final incorruptibility, which permeates the very marrow of the noosphere.

—HM 29–33

CREATIVE UNION:
FROM THE MULTIPLE TO OMEGA

The various principles I have . . . been examining mark out the field within which we must look for a solution of the problem of life — but they do not as yet provide us with an interpretation of the world. This I have tried to work out for myself in the theory of creative union.

Creative union is not exactly a metaphysical doctrine. It is rather a sort of empirical and pragmatic explanation of the universe, conceived in my mind from the need to reconcile in a solidly coherent system scientific views on evolution (accepted as, in their essence, definitively established) with the innate urge that has impelled me to look for the divine not in a cleavage with the physical world but through matter, and, in some sort of way, in union with matter.

I arrived quite simply at this explanation of things by considering the extremely puzzling relationship between spirit and matter. If there is any fact well established by experience, it is that "the higher the level of psychism attained, in all the living beings we know, the more closely it appears to be associated with a complex organism." The more spiritual the soul is, the more multiple and fragile is its body. This curious law of compensation does not seem to have attracted any special attention from the philosophers, except insofar as it has provided them with an opportunity of driving even deeper the abyss they seek to set between spirit and matter. It seemed to me that far from being a paradoxical or accidental relationship, it might very well disclose to us the hidden constitution of beings. Instead, therefore, of treating it as a difficulty or an objection, I transformed it into the very principle by which things may be explained.

Creative union is the theory that accepts this proposition: in the present evolutionary phase of the cosmos (the only phase known to us), everything happens as though the One were formed by successive unifications of the multiple — and as though the One were more perfect, the more perfectly it centralized under itself a larger multiple. For the elements associated by the soul in a body (and thereby raised to a higher degree of being), ... "to be more is to be more fully united with more. For the soul itself, for the principle of unity, ... to be more, is more fully to unite more." For both, to receive or to communicate union is to undergo the creative influence of God, ... "who creates by uniting."

These expressions should be carefully weighed if they are not to be taken in a wrong sense. They do not mean that the One is composed of the multiple, i.e., that it is born from the fusion in itself of the elements it associates (for in that case either it would not be something created — something completely new — or the terms of the multiple would be progressively decreasing, which contradicts our experience). They simply express this fact, that the One appears to us only in the wake of the multiple, dominating the multiple, since its essential and formal act is to unite. — And this allows us, in consequence, to lay down a fundamental principle, as follows: "creative union does not fuse together the terms which it associates (for does not the bliss it confers consist precisely in becoming one with the other while remaining one's own self?). It preserves the terms — it even completes them, as we see in living bodies, where the cells are the more specialized, the higher in the animal series the being to which they belong. Every higher soul *differentiates* more fully the elements it unites." ...

At the lower limit of things, too deep for any of us to penetrate, it discloses an immense plurality — complete diversity combined with total disunity. This absolute multiplicity would, in truth, be nothingness, and it has never existed. But it is the quarter from which the world emerges for us: at the beginning of all time, the world appears to us rising up from the multiple, impregnated with and still bedewed with the multiple. Already, however, since *something* exists, the work of unification has begun. In the first stages in which it becomes conceivable to us, the world has already been for a long time at the mercy of a multitude of elementary souls that fight for its dust in order that, by unifying it, they may exist. There can be no doubt about it — what we call inorganic matter is certainly animate in its own way. Complete exteriority or total "transience," like absolute multiplicity, is synonymous with nothingness. Atoms, electrons, elementary particles, no matter what they be (so long as they are something outside ourselves) must possess the rudiments of immanence; in other words, they must have a spark of spirit. ...

Such, all around us, is the position in the universe. Like a sphere that radiates from innumerable centers, the material world can today be seen by us as suspended from the spiritual consciousness of human beings. What has creative union to teach us about the balance and the future of this system? It gives us formal warning that the world we see is still profoundly unstable and incomplete. Unstable, because the millions of souls (living or departed) now included in the cosmos form an uneasy multiple, that, for mechanical reasons, must have a center if it is to hold together. Incomplete because, while it represents a weakness, their very plurality is a strength and a source of hope for the future — that being the demand for or the anticipation of a later unification in spirit. In consequence, the whole weight of past evolution forces us all to look higher than ourselves in the series of spiritual development. If it is our own souls that give solidity to the infrahuman world, the human world, in turn, cannot be conceived except as supported by conscious centers vaster and more powerful than ours. Thus we are gradually introduced (from the more multiple to the less multiple) to the concept of a first, supreme center, or Omega, in which all the fibers, the threads, the generating lines, of the universe are knit together. From the point of view of the completion of the movement it governs it is a center still in formation — a potential center; but it is already a real center, too, since without its attractive force operating here and now, the general stream of unification would be unable to raise up the multiple.

The picture, then, is perfectly clear: in the light of creative union the universe assumes the form of a huge cone, whose base expands indefinitely to the rear, into darkness, while its apex rises up and concentrates ever further into the light. Throughout the whole, the *same* creative influence makes itself felt, but always in a more conscious, more purified, more complex form.... Science is necessarily chiefly concerned with studying the material arrangements that are successively effected by the progress of life. In so doing, it sees only the outer crust of things. The true evolution of the world takes place in souls and in their union. Its inner factors are not mechanistic but psychological and moral. That, as we shall again have occasion to note, is why the further, physical, developments of humankind — the true continuation, that is, of its planetary, biological, evolution — will be found in the increased consciousness obtained by the activation of psychical forces of unification....

This fundamental principle stands out with all the emphasis of a truth of the first order, that "all consistence comes from spirit." In that we have the very definition of creative union. Our direct, undigested experience of the world would incline us to the contrary view. The solidity of the inorganic and the fragility of the flesh tend to stimulate the belief that all consistence comes from matter. We must resolutely reverse this crude view of things; physics, in fact, is busily abolishing it by demonstrating the slow disappearance of substances that we used to regard as indestructible. The truth is that nothing holds together except as the result of a synthesis, which means, in short, however lowly the synthesis, by a reflection of spirit....

In the system of creative union, it becomes impossible to continue crudely to contrast spirit and matter. For those who have understood the law of "spiritualization by union," there are no longer two compartments in the universe, the spiritual and the physical: there are only *two directions* along one and the same road (the direction of pernicious pluralization and that of beneficial unification). Every being in the world stands somewhere on the slope that rises up from the shadows toward the light. In front of it lies the effort to master and simplify its own nature; behind, the abandonment of effort in the physical and moral disintegration of its powers. If it goes forward, it meets the good: everything is spirit for it. If it falls back, it meets nothing on its road but evil and matter....

Matter and spirit are not opposed as two separate things, as two natures, but as two directions of evolution within the world.   — "My Universe" in SC 44–49, 51

THE FUNDAMENTAL IMPORTANCE OF THE HUMAN PHENOMENON

No sooner has the human being been reintegrated...in the structure of the world than he begins, in the eyes of science, to assume immense value. As soon as he is no longer regarded as a sort of epi- or para-phenomenon, he can only be, both qualitatively and quantitatively, a phenomenon of the first order in the universe....

In the first place *qualitatively,* the human being displays, to a special degree — which makes it easy to study — a certain particular energy in the world, the extreme term, in our experience, of what we might call the psychic current of the universe. Just, for example, as the exceptional intensity of the activity of radium has introduced physics to a universal property of matter, so...consciousness, even in its highest form which is freedom, is seen to be a factor that has cosmic value. Inapprehensible in the world of atoms, negligible at times in the world of organic beings, in the world of the human being the psychic becomes decisively the principal phenomenon. It must, therefore, be accepted by science as a scientific fact. This, it seems, cannot be disputed; and I believe that it would remain demonstrably true, even if the considerations that follow were to be left out of account.

By the very fact that it represents the distinct emergence of a universal property, the human phenomenon acquires an unbounded *quantitative* value....Humanity...evolves in such a way as to form a natural unity whose extension is as vast as the earth. Our concern with the ordinary business of human beings prevents us from appreciating the significance of this tremendous event. And yet it is taking place under our very eyes. From day to day the human mass is "setting"; it is building itself up; it is weaving around the globe a network of material organization, of communication, and of thought. Submerged as we are in this process and accustomed to regard it as nonphysical, we pay little attention to it. Suppose that we at last come to look at it as we would a crystal or a plant: we immediately realize that, through us, the earth *is engaged in adding* to its lithosphere, its atmosphere, its biosphere, and its other layers, one more envelope — the last and the most remarkable of all. This is the thinking zone, the "noosphere." Looked at from the angle of the globally elaborated result of its evolution, the human phenomenon is "telluric" in order. Its spatial dimensions coincide with those of the planet: its temporal dimensions, too. Is not man naturally in solidarity with the earth, has he not authentically emerged from the general history of the earth? The human phenomenon...has enabled science, rather as radioactivity does, to read the secret of the elemental driving forces of the world. We see that it takes on the amplitude (in extension) and the depth (in duration) of geological events. Humankind, to repeat, but with fuller understanding, an expression we have already used earlier, is indeed the "hominized" earth — we might even say "hominized" nature....

Hitherto science has been accustomed to construct the physical world solely from elements that are drawn, by the laws of chance and great numbers, toward an increasing dissipation of interchangeable energies and a state of inorganic diffusion. Once we have decided to see in humankind a physical phenomenon, we are obliged to conceive another fundamental irreversibility running counter to or across this first universal current. This is the irreversibility that leads things, in the opposite direction from the probable, toward ever more improbable and more fully organic constructions. Side by side with the measurable current of entropy, or running across it, there is another current, impatient of measurement; it is disguised in the material, comes to the surface of the organic, but is most clearly visible in the human. This is the imponderable current of spirit....

Two important corollaries would derive from this situation, were it accepted as a fact by science: the first somewhat speculative, the second eminently practical.

Speculatively, we would hold the key (allowing for the necessary analogies) that would allow us to explore from within the universe that physics has, until now, tried to apprehend from without. If it is indeed true, as we have seen, that the laws of inorganic matter and the external processes of living matter can continue upward as far as us and reappear "hominized" in us, it is because we can, conversely, try to understand them both by making our way toward them from within, there to meet ourselves again, materialized....

Practically, we shall find ourselves the responsible trustees of a portion of universal energy that must be conserved and extended — not an indiscriminate energy, but one that has been brought, in us, to a supreme degree of elaboration. However coldly and objectively we may study things, we must still conclude that humanity constitutes a front along which the cosmos advances.

This would in the first place entail for us a new and noble obligation to make all the forces provided by the earth serve to advance the progress of the improbable. However, to harness material energies would still be only a secondary task. If the current of spirit, represented today by humankind, is to continue to flow and to drive ahead, our chief concern would have to be to ensure that the human mass retains its *internal tension:* in other words, it must not allow the respect, the zest, the ardor for life, to run to waste in itself, nor to grow less. If that ardor cools, then what we have called the noosphere immediately withers away and disappears. In this we can get a hint of a new energetics (the maintenance, canalization, and magnification of human aspirations and passions) in which physics, biology, and moral science would all be combined — a surprising combination, indeed, but one that is inevitable as soon as the reality of the human phenomenon has been understood.

I need hardly say that these reflections, which I hope may hasten the time when science will resolutely integrate humankind with the earth and the world, are provisional and no more than a beginning....

After having been regarded for many years as a scientifically subsidiary or anomalous element of the universe, humankind will in the end be recognized as a fundamental phenomenon — *the* supreme phenomenon of nature: that in which, in a unique complexity of material and moral factors, one of the principal acts of universal evolution is not only experienced but lived by us. — "The Phenomenon of Man" in SC 92–97

THE DIVINE MILIEU
AND ITS ATTRIBUTES

The enrichment and ferment of religious thought in our time has undoubtedly been caused by the revelation of the size and the unity of the world all around us and within us. All around us the physical sciences are endlessly extending the abysses of time and space and ceaselessly discerning new relationships between the elements of the universe. Within us a whole world of affinities and interrelated sympathies, as old as the human soul, is being awakened by the stimulus of these great discoveries, and what has hitherto been dreamed rather than experienced is at last taking shape and consistency. Scholarly and discriminating among serious thinkers, simple or didactic among the half-educated, the aspirations toward a vaster and more organic *one,* and the premonitions of unknown forces and their application in new fields, are the same, and are emerging simultaneously on all sides. It is almost a commonplace today to find people who, quite naturally and unaffectedly, live in the explicit consciousness of being an atom or a citizen of the universe.

This collective awakening, similar to that which, at some given moment, makes each individual realize the true dimensions of his own life, must inevitably have a profound religious reaction on the mass of humankind — either to cast down or to exalt.

To some, the world has disclosed itself as too vast: within such immensity, the human being is lost and no longer counts; and there is nothing left for him to do but shut his eyes and disappear. To others, on the contrary, the world is too beautiful; and it, and it alone, must be adored.

There are Christians... who remain unaffected by these feelings of anxiety or fascination.... But there are others who are alarmed by the agitation or the attraction invincibly produced in them by this new rising star. Is the Christ of the Gospels, imagined and loved within the dimensions of a Mediterranean world, capable of still embracing and still forming the center of our prodigiously expanded universe? Is the world not in the process of becoming more vast, more close, more dazzling than Jehovah? Will it not burst our religion asunder? Eclipse our God?

Without daring, perhaps, to admit to this anxiety yet, there are many (as I know from having come across them all over the world) who nevertheless feel it deep within them. It is for those that I am writing.

I shall not attempt to embark on metaphysics or apologetics. Instead, I shall turn back, with those who care to follow me, to the Agora. There, in each other's company, we shall listen to St. Paul telling the Areopagites of "God, who made human beings so that we might seek him — God whom we try to apprehend by the groping of our lives — that self-same God is as pervasive and perceptible as the atmosphere in which we are bathed. He encompasses us on all sides, like the world itself. What prevents you, then, from enfolding him in your arms? Only one thing: your inability *to see him*."

These pages do no more than recapitulate the eternal lesson of the Church in the words of a man who, because he believes himself to feel deeply in tune with his own times, has sought to teach how to see God everywhere, to see him in all that is most hidden, most solid, and most ultimate in the world. These pages put forward no more than a practical attitude — or, more exactly perhaps, a way of teaching how to see.... Place yourself here, where I am, and look from this privileged position — which is no hard-won height reserved for the elect, but the solid platform built by two thousand years of Christian experience — and you will see how easily the two stars, whose divergent attractions were disorganizing your faith, are brought into conjunction. Without mixture, without confusion, the true God, the Christian God, will under your gaze invade the universe, our universe of today, the universe which so frightened you by its alarming size or its pagan beauty. He will penetrate it as a ray of light does a crystal and, with the help of the great layers of creation, he will become for you universally perceptible and active — very near and very distant at one and the same time.

If you are able to focus your soul's eyes so as to perceive this magnificence, you will soon forget, I assure you, your unfounded fears in face of the mounting significance of the earth. Your one thought will be to exclaim: "Greater still, Lord, let your universe be greater still, so that I may hold you and be held by you by a contact at once made ever more intense and ever wider in its extent!" ...

The essential marvel of the divine milieu is the ease with which it assembles and harmonizes within itself qualities which appear to us to be contradictory.

As vast as the world and much more formidable than the most immense energies of the universe, it nevertheless possesses in a supreme degree that precise concentrated particularity that makes up so much of the warm charm of human persons.

Vast and innumerable as the dazzling surge of creatures that are sustained and sur-animated by its ocean, it nevertheless retains the concrete transcendence that allows it to bring back the elements of the world, without the least confusion, within its triumphant and personal unity.

Incomparably near and perceptible — for it presses in upon us through all the forces of the universe — it nevertheless eludes our grasp so constantly that we can never seize it here below except by raising ourselves, uplifted on its waves, to the extreme limit of our effort: present in, and drawing at the inaccessible depth of, each creature, it withdraws always further, bearing us along with it toward the common center of all consummation. ...

Now, if we try to discover the source of so many astonishingly coupled perfections, we shall find they all spring from the same "fontal" property which we can express thus: God reveals himself everywhere, beneath our groping efforts, as a *universal milieu*, only because he is the *ultimate point* upon which all realities converge.... It follows that all created things, every one of them, cannot be looked at, in their nature and actions, without the same reality being found in their innermost being — like sunlight in the fragments of a broken mirror — one beneath its multiplicity, unattainable beneath its proximity, and spiritual beneath its materiality. No object can influence us by its essence without our being touched by the radiance of the focus of the universe. Our minds are incapable of grasping a reality, our hearts and hands of seizing the essentially desirable in it, without our being compelled *by the very structure of things* to go back to the first source of its perfections. This focus, this source, is thus everywhere. It is *precisely because* he is at once so deep and yet so akin to an extensionless point that God is infinitely near and dispersed everywhere. It is *precisely because* he is the center that he fills the whole sphere. The omnipresence of the divine is simply the effect of its extreme spirituality and is the exact contrary of the fallacious ubiquity which matter seems to derive from its extreme dissociation and dispersal. In the light of this discovery, we may resume our march through the inexhaustible wonders which the divine milieu has in store for us.

However vast the divine milieu may be, it is in reality a *center*. It therefore has the properties of a center and above all the absolute and final power to unite (and consequently to complete) all beings within its breast. In the divine milieu all the elements of the universe *touch each other* by that which is most inward and ultimate in them. There they concentrate, little by little, all that is purest and most attractive in them without loss and without danger of subsequent corruption. There they shed, in their meeting, the mutual externality and the incoherences which form the basic pain of human relationships. Let those seek refuge there who are saddened by the separations, the meannesses, and the wastefulness of the world. In the external spheres of the world the human is always torn by the separations which set distance between bodies, which set the impossibility of mutual understanding between souls, which set death between lives. Moreover at every minute he must lament that he cannot pursue and embrace everything within the compass of a few years. Finally, and not without reason, he is incessantly distressed by the crazy indifference and the heartbreaking dumbness of a natural environment in which the greater part of individual endeavor seems wasted or lost, where the blow and the cry seem stifled on the spot, without awakening any echo.

All that desolation is only on the surface.

But let us leave the surface and, without leaving the world, plunge into God. There, and from there, in him and through him, we shall hold all things and have command of all things. There we shall one day rediscover the essence and brilliance of all the flowers and lights which we were forced to abandon so as to be faithful to life. The beings we despaired of reaching and influencing are all there, all reunited by the most vulnerable, receptive, and enriching point in their substance. In this place the least of our desires and efforts is harvested and tended and can at any moment cause the marrow of the universe to vibrate.

Let us establish ourselves in the divine milieu. There we shall find ourselves where the soul is most deep and where matter is most dense. There we shall discover, where all its beauties flow together, the ultra-vital, the ultra-sensitive, the ultra-active point of the universe. And, at the same time, we shall feel the *plenitude* of our powers of action and adoration effortlessly ordered within our deepest selves....

To have access to the divine milieu is to have found the one thing needful: *him who burns* by setting fire to everything that we would love badly or not enough; *him who calms* by eclipsing with his blaze everything that we would love too much; *him who consoles* by gathering up everything that has been snatched from our love or has never been given to it. To reach those priceless layers is to experience, with equal truth, that one has need of everything and that one has need of nothing. Everything is needed because the world will never be large enough to provide our taste for action with the means of grasping God, or our thirst for undergoing with the possibility of being invaded by him. And yet nothing is needed; for as the only reality which can satisfy us lies beyond the transparencies in which it is mirrored, everything that fades away and dies between us will only serve to give reality back to us with greater purity. Everything means both everything and nothing to me; everything is God to me and everything is dust to me: that is what a person can say with equal truth, in accord with how the divine ray falls.

— MD 13–16, 100–103, 108–9

THE DIVINIZATION OF ACTIVITIES

We may, perhaps, imagine that the creation was finished long ago. But that would be quite wrong. It continues still more magnificently, and at the highest levels of the world. And we serve to complete it, even by the humblest work of our hands. That is, ultimately, the meaning and value of our acts. Owing to the interrelation between matter, soul, and Christ, we bring part of the being which he desires back to God *in whatever we do*. With each one of our *works*, we labor — in individual separation, but no less really — to build the *pleroma;* that is to say, we bring to Christ a little fulfillment.

Each one of our works, by its more or less remote or direct effect upon the spiritual world, helps to make perfect Christ in his mystical totality. That is the fullest possible answer to the question: How can we, following the call of St. Paul, see God in all the active half of our lives? In fact, through the unceasing operation of the incarnation, the divine so thoroughly permeates all our creaturely energies that, in order to meet it and lay hold on it, we could not find a more fitting setting than that of our action.

To begin with, in action I adhere to the creative power of God; I coincide with it; I become not only its instrument but its living extension. And as there is nothing more personal in a being than his will, I merge myself, in a sense, through my heart, with the very heart of God. This commerce is continuous because I am always acting; and at the same time, since I can never see a boundary to the perfection of my fidelity nor to the fervor of my intention, this commerce enables me to liken myself, ever more strictly and indefinitely, to God.

The soul does not pause to relish this communion, nor does it lose sight of the material end of its action; for it is wedded to a *creative* effort. The will to succeed, a certain passionate delight in the work to be done, form an integral part of our creaturely fidelity. It follows that the very sincerity with which we desire and pursue success for God's sake reveals itself as a new factor — also without limits — in our being knit together with him who animates us. Originally we had fellowship with God in the simple common exercise of wills; but now we unite ourselves with him in the shared love of the end for which we are working; and the crowning marvel is that, with the possession of this end, we have the utter joy of discovering his presence once again. . . .

God, in all that is most living and incarnate in him, is not far away from us, altogether apart from the world we see, touch, hear, smell, and taste about us. Rather he awaits us every instant in our action, in the work of the moment. There is a sense in which he is at the tip of my pen, my spade, my brush, my needle — of my heart and of my thought. By pressing the stroke, the line, or the stitch on which I am engaged to its ultimate natural finish, I shall lay hold of that last end toward which my innermost will tends. Like those formidable physical forces which human beings contrive to discipline so as to make them perform operations of prodigious delicacy, so the tremendous power of the divine attraction is focused on our frail desires and microscopic intents without breaking their point. It sur-animates; hence it neither disturbs anything nor stifles anything. It sur-animates; hence it introduces a higher principle of unity into our spiritual life, the specific effect of which is — depending upon the point of view one adopts — either to make human endeavor holy or to give the Christian life the full flavor of humanity. . . .   — MD 34–37

THE DIVINIZATION OF PASSIVITIES

The passivities of our lives . . . form half of human existence. The term means, quite simply, that that which is not done by us is, by definition, undergone.

But this does not in any way prejudge the proportions in which action and passion possess our inner realm. In fact, these two parts of our lives — the active and the passive — are extraordinarily unequal. Seen from our point of view, the active occupies first place because we prefer it and because it is more easily perceived. But in the reality of things the passive is immeasurably the wider and the deeper part.

In the first place the passivities ceaselessly accompany our conscious deeds, in the form of reactions which direct, sustain, or oppose our efforts. On this ground alone they inevitably and precisely coincide with the scope of our activities. But their sphere of influence extends far beyond these narrow limits. . . .

On one side are the friendly and favorable forces, those which uphold our endeavor and point the way to success — the "passivities of growth." On the other side are the hostile powers which laboriously obstruct our tendencies, hamper or deflect our progress toward heightened being, and thwart our real or apparent capacities for development: these are "passivities of diminishment."...

Growth seems so natural to us that we do not, as a matter of fact, pause to separate from our action the forces which nourish that action or the circumstances which favor its success. And yet...what does thou possess that thou has not previously received? We undergo life as much as we undergo death, if not more.

We must try to penetrate our most secret self and examine our being from all sides. Let us try, patiently, to perceive the ocean of forces to which we are subjected and in which our growth is, as it were, steeped. This is a salutary exercise; for the depth and universality of our dependence on so much altogether outside our control all go to make up the embracing intimacy of our communion with the world to which we belong....

The life of each one of us is, as it were, woven of those two threads: the thread of inward development, through which our ideas and affections and our human and religious attitudes are gradually formed; and the thread of outward success by which we always find ourselves at the exact point where the whole sum of the forces of the universe meet together to work in us the effect which God desires....

To cleave to God hidden beneath the inward and outward forces which animate our being and sustain it in its development is ultimately to open ourselves to, and put trust in, all the breaths of life. We answer to and "communicate" with the passivities of growth by our fidelity in action. Hence by our very desire to experience God passively we find ourselves brought back to the lovable duty of growth.

The moment has come to plumb the decidedly negative side of our existences — the side on which, however far we search, we cannot discern any happy result or any solid conclusion to what happens to us. It is easy enough to understand that God can be grasped in and through every life. But can God also be found in and through every death? This is what perplexes us deeply. And yet this is what we must learn to acknowledge as a matter of settled habit and practice, unless we abandon all that is most characteristically Christian in the Christian outlook, and unless we are prepared to forfeit commerce with God in one of the most widespread and at the same time most profoundly passive and receptive experiences of human life.

The forces of diminishment are our real passivities. Their number is vast, their forms infinitely varied, their influence constant. In order to clarify our ideas and direct our meditation we will divide them into two groups corresponding to the two forms under which we considered the forces of growth: the diminishments whose origin lies *within us,* and the diminishments whose origin lies *outside us.*

The external passivities of diminishment are all our bits of ill fortune. We have only to look back on our lives to see them springing up on all sides: the barrier which blocks our way, the wall that hems us in, the stone which throws us from our path, the obstacle that breaks us, the invisible microbe that kills the body, the little word that infects the mind, all the incidents and accidents of varying importance and varying kinds, the tragic interferences (upsets, shocks, severances, deaths) which come between the world of "other" things and the world that radiates out from us. And yet when hail, fire, and thieves had taken everything from Job — all his wealth and all his family — Satan could say to God: "Skin for skin, and all that a man hath he will give for his life. But put forth thy hand, and touch his bone and his flesh: and then thou shalt see that he will curse thee to thy face." In a sense the loss of things means little to us because we can always imagine getting them back. What is terrible for us is to be cut off from things through some inward diminishment that can never be retrieved.

Humanly speaking, the internal passivities of diminishment form the darkest elements and the most despairingly useless years of our life. Some were waiting to pounce on us as we first awoke: natural failings, physical defects, intellectual or moral weaknesses, as a result of which the field of our activities, of our enjoyment, of our vision, has been pitilessly limited since birth. Others were lying in wait for us later on and appeared as suddenly and brutally as an accident or as stealthily as an illness. All of us one day or another will come to realize, if we have not already done so, that one or other of these sources of disintegration has lodged itself in the very heart of our lives. Sometimes it is the cells of the body that rebel or become diseased; at other times the very elements of our personality seem to be in conflict or to detach themselves from any sort of order. And then we impotently stand by and watch collapse, rebellion, and inner tyranny, and no friendly influence can come to our help. And if by chance we escape, to a greater or lesser extent, the critical forms of these assaults from without which appear deep within us and irresistibly destroy the strength, the light, and the love by which we live, there still remains that slow, essential deterioration which we cannot escape: old age little by little robbing us of ourselves and pushing us on toward the end. Time, which postpones possession, time, which tears us away from enjoyment, time, which condemns us all to death — what a formidable passivity is the passage of time....

In death, as in an ocean, all our slow or swift diminishments flow out and merge. Death is the sum and consummation of all our diminishments....

We must overcome death by finding God in it. And by the same token, we shall find the divine established in our innermost hearts, in the last stronghold which might have seemed able to escape his reach.

Here again, as in the case of the "divinization" of our human activities, we shall find the Christian faith absolutely explicit in what it claims to be the case and what it bids us do. Christ has conquered death, not only by suppressing its evil effects, but by reversing its sting. By virtue of Christ's rising again, nothing any longer kills inevitably, but everything is capable of becoming the blessed touch of the divine hands, the blessed influence of the will of God upon our lives. However marred by our faults or however desperate in its circumstances our position may be, we can, by a total reordering, completely correct the world that surrounds us and resume our lives in a favorable sense. *Diligentibus Deum omnia convertuntur in bonum.* That is the fact which dominates all explanation and all discussion.

—MD 52–54, 58–61

THE MASS ON THE WORLD

Since once again, Lord...I have neither bread, nor wine, nor altar, I will raise myself beyond these symbols, up to the pure majesty of the real itself; I, your priest, will make the whole earth my altar and on it will offer you all the labors and sufferings of the world.

Over there, on the horizon, the sun has just touched with light the outermost fringe of the eastern sky. Once again, beneath this moving sheet of fire, the living surface of the earth wakes and trembles, and once again begins its fearful travail. I will place on my paten, O God, the harvest to be won by this renewal of labor. Into my chalice I shall pour all the sap which is to be pressed out this day from the earth's fruits.

My paten and my chalice are the depths of a soul laid widely open to all the forces which in a moment will rise up from every corner of the earth and converge upon the Spirit. Grant me the remembrance and the mystic presence of all those whom the light is now awakening to the new day.

One by one, Lord, I see and I love all those whom you have given me to sustain and charm my life. One by one also I number all those who make up that other beloved family which has gradually surrounded me, its unity fashioned out of the most disparate elements, with affinities of the heart, of scientific research, and of thought. And again one by one — more vaguely it is true, yet all-inclusively — I call before me the whole vast anonymous army of living humanity; those who surround me and support me though I do not know them; those who come and those who go; above all, those who in office, laboratory, and factory, through their vision of truth or despite their error, truly believe in the progress of earthly reality and who today will take up again their impassioned pursuit of the light.

This restless multitude, confused or orderly, the immensity of which terrifies us; this ocean of humanity whose slow, monotonous wave-flows trouble the hearts even of those whose faith is most firm: it is to this deep that I thus desire all the fibers of my being should respond. All the things in the world to which this day will bring increase; all those that will diminish; all those too that will die: all of them, Lord, I try to gather into my arms, so as to hold them out to you in offering. This is the material of my sacrifice, the only material you desire.

Once upon a time men took into your temple the first fruits of their harvests, the flower of their flocks. But the offering you really want, the offering you mysteriously need every day to appease your hunger, to slake your thirst is nothing less than the growth of the world borne ever onward in the stream of universal becoming.

Receive, O Lord, this all-embracing host which your whole creation, moved by your magnetism, offers you at this dawn of a new day.

This bread, our toil, is of itself, I know, but an immense fragmentation; this wine, our pain, is no more, I know, than a drought that dissolves. Yet in the very depths of this formless mass you have implanted — and this I am sure of, for I sense it — a desire, irresistible, hallowing, which makes us cry out, believer and unbeliever alike: "Lord, make us *one*."

—*The Mass on the World* in HM 119–21.

Chapter 3

Christ in All Things

Clothed in the glory of the world.
—MD 118

Teilhard's faith was thoroughly incarnational and thoroughly christocentric. He attached a realism to the doctrine of the incarnation which is rare. As a scientist he studied the evolution of the earth, the organic development of living forms, and the origin of human beings, all of which required a keen eye for concrete details and continuous contact with the living world. His "seeing," so often mentioned in his writings, was rooted in the experience of the senses, in touching and tasting, which nourished his inner perception of the spiritual essence of things. For him, Christians need to be animated and fired by a "cosmic consciousness" which meets God through the abundant, beautiful, and awesome realities of the earth, even though God is also distinct from creation. For Teilhard, the figure of Jesus Christ is not only human and divine, but also cosmic, for Christ's influence and presence can be found in all things in the world and in the cosmos.

At first, Teilhard described Christ, or "the Christic," as a "universal element" present everywhere through God's creative action, but Christ is also the organic center of the entire cosmos, its heart, and "the soul of the world." The whole cosmic process of evolution is linked to increasing centering and convergence, and Teilhard sees this process as culminating in a final center which he calls "Omega." Furthermore, this center which meets the yearnings of science, becomes in the eyes of his Christian faith expanded into "Christ-Omega" or the "universal Christ," the organic, dynamic, deeply personal and fiery center of love in the universe, the point of convergence for all things and people.

This is the Christ whose heart takes on the dimension of the universe, whose life and spiritual energies pulsate through it like a blazing fire. Teilhard imaginatively draws out the convergence of all things in Christ-Omega or "Super-Christ" on such a magnificent scale that some may find it almost too dazzlingly speculative. His vision is not an easy intellectual synthesis, as many essays in the collection Science and Christ show; yet it is a profoundly existential and mystical insight which can inspire love and communion with God through the universe. Christ-Omega as a historical, personal, and cosmic reality, symbolized by the image of the heart as a furnace of fire, of energy, life, and light — this is the incarnate God Teilhard worshiped and asks us to adore.

Teilhard's love of the heart of Jesus draws on traditional beliefs and devotions, but these were reinterpreted by him in a new and original manner as he explained in his autobiographical essay "The Heart of Matter" (1950), written toward the end of his life. But this love found expression from the beginning of his writing. Nowhere is the lyrical quality of his intimate love for the incarnate, cosmic Christ more beautifully described than in the early essay "Christ in the World of Matter" (1916, reproduced in WTW, HU, and HM), most of which is reproduced below. Speaking through the voice of a friend, Teilhard most probably here describes one of his own important mystical experiences. It focuses on the picture representing "Christ offering his heart" on the walls of a church where he had gone to pray. Suddenly the outlines of the individual figure of the human Jesus shown in the painting were melting away and radiating

*outward toward infinity, so that the entire universe was per-
ceived as contained within this heart vibrant with movement,
energy, and love. Teilhard describes Christ's garment and gaze,
the beauty of his eyes, their expression of both immense joy and
suffering. It was in the sacred heart of Jesus that the conjunction of the divine and cosmic, of spirit and matter, occurred for
him, as he wrote in his diary at that time.*

   *God's omnipresence in the universe is revealed to us through
the incarnation, a still ongoing event wherein Christ's body
continues to grow to ever larger stature. The mystical, divine
milieu that surrounds us, that we breathe in and can communicate with, is still expanding, intensifying, disclosing itself in the
"ever-greater Christ" whose praise Teilhard's prayers put into
words of surrender, prayerful union, and adoration. Our universe is a christified universe, marked by divine omnipresence
shining through both the glory and the pain of the world. Christ
is the center of the universe, he is the center of humanity, he is
the center of every human being. Teilhard considered it his life's
vocation to be at the service of this universal Christ. When he
died, a picture of the radiant heart of Christ was found on his
desk, inscribed with a litany addressed to the heart of God, the
heart of Jesus, the heart of the world — a final testimony to a
powerful mystical vision of great intensity and splendor.* *

CHRIST AS UNIVERSAL ELEMENT

The Christian who is animated by cosmic consciousness must
hold above all else that God, the only Absolute, is essentially
distinct from creation.

   Nevertheless, if he is to be *able* to love and worship God
"with all his heart" he has a need that will take no denial to
apprehend the divinity under the form of a universal element.

---

*The text of the litany can be found in CE 244f.

What physical relation, between the transcendent Absolute and the universe, what emanation or influence, can he find that will satisfy, without doing violence to his faith, his impassioned vision of supreme "cosmic" reality, present in all things? How can he reconcile in his mind the law of his Church and the law of his heart?

Let me point out three successive stages which I *myself in real fact went through*, before I arrived at a satisfactory solution of this interior problem of making one's way to God *in all the sincerity and fullness of a soul that is irrevocably "cosmic."*

1. The first "universal reality" that offered itself to my mind, in the domain of divino-terrestrial forces, was the will of God, conceived as a special energy instilled into beings to animate them and order them toward their end.

If the will of God is seen with sufficient intensity and realism it positively transforms the universe. It animates and softens all that we suffer; it stimulates and directs all that we initiate; it abolishes chance. It makes it possible for us to live, physically and forever, within the divine unity: that unity comes to us through all the influences to which we are subject — and we, in turn, through our obedience, become the instruments, we become an extension of, even members of, that unity.

For a long time this was the only vision that filled my life, as giving me God, universally immediate and tangible.

Gradually, however, I came to feel that the divine presence of which I was thus assured did not come up to the measure of my experience or satisfy my desires. I was eager for something more — and I felt that *there must be something more —* in the universe, between God and myself, than a perpetual and universal contact in self-surrender and action.

Through the will of God, universally seen and apprehended, I was becoming (and all things were becoming for me) *instruments* of God. What I wanted was to see that I was in some way, in virtue of my religious faith, an *element* of God — and to see all things share that quality with me.

2. Thus I found it necessary to give greater precision to my first approximate explanation of the dogma and of my own instinct, and so to accept *God's creative action* as the universal element.

In that new form, I could already see God as entering the sphere of external experience in which we move. Animating the great natural currents of life and matter, he penetrated into my own personal essence and into the development and growth of all things. He was the soul of everything that moves, the support of everything that exists. This stage corresponded more or less exactly to the views developed by St. Ignatius in his meditation *ad amorem.*

Here again, however, I soon came to feel that something was lacking in the terms I was using to express the reality, the intimate quality, of the universal presence experienced.

Even when seen as the supreme cause, God was still too separate from the world to satisfy me. Even when involved in his creative action, I was still not, in relation to God, the extremely lowly *element* that I felt myself to be — that I wished to be. And, on his side, God was till not the higher element, infused into the universe, through which the Absolute entered into my body and spirit.

For all God's intermixture with my being through his almighty action, there still remained between him and me a hiatus, a void, an icy gap, representing the distance that separates necessary from participated being. I felt that I *was not united* to him but *juxtaposed.*

3. It was only after writing an essay entitled "The Mystical Milieu" that I arrived at a conclusive explanation of what I felt. At last I found within myself the name that Christianity gives to the universal reality I had worshiped so long: it was *"the cosmic influence* [life] *of Christ."*

However, before explaining this unusual expression, I must add a comment of the philosophical order on the way in which we should conceive individuals in the universe.

As a result of the more restricted necessities of practical life, we have become accustomed to considering persons (monads) as the natural, complete, units into which the world can be broken down. When we speak of "a soul," we believe that we are thinking of an independent reality, coterminous with itself, separable *in its identity* from other souls and even from the universe. This pluralist concept may well be most inaccurate.

Certain though it is that Peter and Paul are two definitively separate and contrastable beings, *so long as we remain on the social plane of present-day humankind,* it is equally probable that if we consider them as situated *in the total universe,* neither of them can attain his full personality, his full significance, his full determination, except within the general design of the world. And this probability would become a certainty, if we knew that, in virtue of its nature, the universe was moving toward a *total end.* If such an end does in fact exist, then every being (inasmuch as it is *essentially* an element of such a universe) has its own particular essence crowned by a certain quality, a certain *form* (common to all) which makes it an integral, rightly adapted, part of the single whole with which it shares a natural harmony.... We must say of every man that he contains in himself, besides a body and a soul, a certain physical entity that relates him in his entirety to the universe (the final universe) in which he reaches his fulfillment.

This is because, strictly speaking, there is in the universe only one single individuality (one single monad), that of the whole (conceived in its organized plurality). The unity or measure of the world is the world itself.

Once we have understood the nature of this *"cosmic composition" of created being,* and have appreciated the closeness and universality of the ties it forms with the multiple, Christ's features take on an extraordinary sharpness and immediacy — and the meaning of Scripture is given incomparable clarity and depth.

We know from what St. Paul and St. John tell us that Christ

is the center of creation, the force that can subject all things to itself, the endpoint by which all things are informed.

What can we learn from those names given to Christ, if we look back at what we have just been saying?

The answer is unmistakable: that in every creature there exists physically (in virtue of Christ's having been chosen to be the head of the universe), *besides* the individual material and spiritual characteristics we recognize in it, a certain relationship that *all being* has to Christ — a particular adaptation to Christ of created essence — *something of Christ*, in short that is born and develops, and gives the whole individual (even the "natural" individual) its ultimate personality and final ontological value.

In virtue of even the natural properties of the universal center, the mystical body of Christ is haloed by a *cosmic body*, that is to say, by *all things* inasmuch as they are drawn by Christ to converge upon him and so reach their fulfillment in him, in the *pleroma*. We can live and act, immersed forever in this living atmosphere coextensive with the world. It is through and within the organic unity of the total Christ, it is under his *formal* influx, that God's will and his creative action finally come through to us and make us one with him.

In our world, when it is supernaturalized, the universal element is ultimately Christ, inasmuch as everything is integrated and consummated within it. It is the living *form* of the incarnate Word, universally attainable and perfectible.

With ever the same brilliance in all, Christ shines as a light at the heart, to which none can ever penetrate, of every life, at the ideal end of *every* growth. Everywhere he draws us to him and brings us closer to himself, in a universal movement of convergence toward spirit. It is he *alone* whom we seek and in whom we move. But if we are to hold him we must take *all things* to, and even beyond, the utmost limit of their nature and their capacity for progress.

Of the cosmic Christ, we may say both that he is and that he is still growing.

He has already appeared in the world; but a long process of growth awaits him in this world, either individuals taken separately — or still more, perhaps, in a *certain human spiritual unity,* of which our present society is no more than an adumbration.

— "The Universal Element" in WTW 294–98

ATTRIBUTES OF THE UNIVERSAL CHRIST

By the universal Christ, I mean Christ the organic center of the entire universe.

Organic center: that is to say, the center on which even every natural development is ultimately physically dependent.

Of the entire universe: that is to say, the center not only of the earth and humankind, but of Sirius and Andromeda, of the angels, of all the realities on which we are physically dependent, whether in a close or a distant relationship (and that, in all probability, means the center of all participated being).

Of the entire universe, again, that is to say, the center not only of moral and religious effort, but also of all that that effort implies — in other words of all physical and spiritual growth.

This universal Church is the Christ presented to us in the Gospels, and more particularly by St. Paul and St. John. It is the Christ by whom the great mystics lived: but nevertheless not the Christ with whom theology has been most concerned.

In the first place, faced by the physical immensity that is thus revealed to our generation, some (the unbelievers) turn away from Christ a priori, because an image of him is often presented to them that is manifestly more insignificant than the world. Others, better informed (and this includes many believers), nevertheless feel that a fight to the death is going on within them. *Which will be the greater* they will have to face and which, therefore, will command their worship — Christ or the universe? The latter is continually growing greater, beyond all measure. It is absolutely essential that the former should be officially, and explicitly, set above all measure.

If the unbelievers are to begin to believe, and the believers to continue to do so, we must hold up . . . the figure of the universal Christ.

Has it been noted that, as the universe is seen to be more immense in its determinism, its past, and its extension, so those attributes become an uncommonly heavy burden for our classical philosophy and theology? Under the constant flood of being that science lets loose, a certain small-scale academic Christ is swept away; and instead the great Christ of tradition and mysticism is revealed and must be accepted: and it is to this Christ that we must turn.

In studying the universal Christ we do more than offer the world, whether believing or unbelieving, a more attractive figure. We impose upon theology (dogmatic, mystical, moral) a complete recasting.

If Christ is to be truly universal, the redemption, and hence the fall, must extend to the whole universe. Original sin accordingly takes on a *cosmic nature* that tradition has always accorded to it, but which, in view of the new dimensions we recognize in our universe, obliges us radically to restate the historical representation of that sin and the too purely juridical way in which we commonly describe its being passed on.

If Christ is universal (if, in other words, he is gradually consummated from all created being) it follows that his kingdom, in its essence, goes beyond the domain of the life that is, in a strict sense, called supernatural. Human action can be related to Christ, and can cooperate in the fulfillment of Christ, not only by the intention, the fidelity, and the obedience in which — as an addition — it is clothed, but also by the actual *material content* of the work done. All progress, whether in organic life or in scientific knowledge, in aesthetic faculties or in social consciousness, can therefore be made Christian. . . . To realize this very simple fact is to tear down the distressing barrier that, *in spite of everything, still stands,* in our present theorizing, between Christian and human effort. Human effort becomes divinizable,...and so for the Christian the world becomes divine in its entirety. The whole of our ascetical and mystical doctrine is thereby given a new vitality.

—"Note on the Universal Christ" in SC 14–17

•

The question of Christ himself — who is he? Turn to the most weighty and most unmistakable passages in the Scriptures. Question the Church about her most essential beliefs, and this is what you will learn: Christ is not something added to the world as an extra, he is not an embellishment, a king as we now crown kings, the owner of a great estate....He is the Alpha and the Omega, the principle and the end, the foundation stone and the keystone, the Plenitude and the Plenifier. He is the one who consummates all things and gives them their consistence. It is toward him and through him, the inner life and light of the world, that the universal convergence of all created spirit is effected in sweat and tears. He is the single center, precious and consistent, who glitters at the summit that is to crown the world, at the opposite pole from those dim and eternally shrinking regions into which our science ventures when it descends the road of matter and the past....

We Christians have no need to be afraid of, or to be unreasonably shocked by, the results of scientific research, whether in physics, in biology, or in history. Some Catholics are disconcerted when it is pointed out to them either that the laws of providence may be reduced to determinism and chance or that under our most spiritual powers there lie hidden most complex material structures, or that the Christian religion has roots in a natural religious development of human consciousness, or that the human body presupposes a vast series of previous organic developments. Such Catholics either deny the facts or are afraid to face them. This is a huge mistake. The analyses of science and history are very often accurate, but they detract nothing from the almighty power of God nor from the spirituality of the soul nor from the supernatural character of Christianity. . . .

Thus science should not disturb our faith by its analyses. Rather, it should help us to know God better, to understand and appreciate him more fully. Personally, I am convinced that there is no more substantial nourishment for the religious life than contact with scientific realities, if they are properly understood. The person who habitually lives in the society of the elements of this world, who personally experiences the overwhelming immensity of things and their wretched dissociation, that person, I am certain, becomes more acutely conscious than anyone of the tremendous need for the unity that continually drives the universe further ahead, and of the fantastic future that awaits it. No one understands so fully as the person who is absorbed in the study of matter to what a degree Christ, through his incarnation, is interior to the world, rooted in the world even in the heart of the tiniest atom. . . .

It is useless, in consequence, and it is unfair, to oppose science and Christ, or to separate them as two domains alien to one another. By itself, science cannot discover Christ, but Christ satisfies the yearnings that are born in our hearts in the school of science.   — "Science and Christ" in SC 34–36

SUPER-CHRIST AND CHRIST-OMEGA

Let us now completely reverse the perspective: by that I mean that after trying to advance from the bottom to the top along the experimental roads opened up by science, let us look at things from the top downward, starting from the peaks to which we are raised by Christianity and religion.

By Super-Christ I most certainly do not mean *another* Christ, a second Christ different from and greater than the first. I mean *the same* Christ, the Christ of all time, revealing himself to us in a form and in dimensions, with an urgency and area of contact, that are enlarged and given new force....

Christ coincides...with what I earlier called Omega point.

Christ, therefore, possesses all the superhuman attributes of Omega point....

The universal Christic center, determined by theology, and the universal cosmic center postulated by anthropogenesis: these two focal points ultimately coincide (or at least overlap) in the historical setting in which we are contained. Christ would not be the sole mover, the sole outcome, of the universe if it were possible for the universe in any way to integrate itself, even to a lesser degree, apart from Christ. And even more certainly, Christ, it would seem, would have been physically incapable of supernaturally centering the universe upon himself if it had not provided the incarnation with a specially favored point at which, in virtue of their natural structure, all the strands of the cosmos tend to meet together. It is therefore toward Christ, in fact, that we turn our eyes when, however approximate our concept of it may be, we look ahead toward a higher pole of humanization and personalization.

In position and function, Christ, here and now, fills for us the place of Omega point....

In spite of the repeated assertions of St. Paul and the Greek Fathers, Christ's universal power over creation has hitherto been considered by theologians primarily in an extrinsic and juridical aspect. "Christ is king of the world, because his Father *declared* him to be king. He is master of all because all has been given to him." That is about as far as the teachers in Israel went, or were prepared to venture, in their explanations of the dogma. Except in regard to the mysterious "sanctifying grace," the organic side of the incarnation, and in consequence its physical presuppositions or conditions, were relegated to the background: the more readily so, in that the recent and terrifying increased dimensions of our universe (in volume, duration, and number) seemed finally to make physical control of the cosmic totality by the person Christ inconceivable.

All these improbabilities disappear and St. Paul's boldest sayings readily take on a literal meaning as soon as the world is seen to be suspended, by its conscious side, from an Omega point of convergence, and Christ, in virtue of his incarnation, is recognized as carrying out precisely the functions of Omega.

If Christ does indeed hold the position of Omega in the heaven of our universe (and this is perfectly possible, since, structurally, Omega is superpersonal in nature) then a whole series of remarkable properties become the prerogative of his risen humanity.

In the first place, he is physically and literally, *he who fills all things:* at no instant in the world is there any element of the world that has moved, that moves, that ever shall move, outside the directing flood he pours into them. Space and duration are filled by him.

Again physically and literally, he is he who *consummates:* the plenitude of the world being finally effected only in the final synthesis in which a supreme consciousness will appear upon total, supremely organized, complexity. And since he, Christ, is the organic principle of this harmonizing process, the whole universe is *ipso facto* stamped with his character, shaped according to his direction, and animated by his form.

Finally, and once more physically and literally, since all the structural lines of the world converge upon him and are knitted together in him, it is he who *gives its consistence* to the entire edifice of matter and spirit. . . .

We see, then, that there is indeed no exaggeration in using the term "Super-Christ" to express that excess of greatness assumed in our consciousness by the person of Christ in step with the awakening of our minds to the super-dimensions of the world and of humankind.

It is not, I insist, another Christ: it is the same Christ, still and always the same, and even more so in that it is precisely in order to retain for him his essential property of being *coextensive with the world* that we are obliged to make him undergo this colossal magnification.

Christ-Omega: the Christ, therefore, who animates and gathers up all the biological and spiritual energies developed by the universe. Finally, then, Christ the evolver.

It is in that form then, now clearly defined and all-embracing, that Christ the Redeemer and Savior henceforth offers himself for our worship....

— "Super-Humanity, Super-Christ, Super-Charity"
in SC 164–67

•

Let us...give the name of Omega to the upper cosmic goal disclosed by creative union. All that I shall have to say about it may be reduced to three points:

A. The revealed Christ is identical with Omega.

B. It is inasmuch as he is Omega that he is seen to be attainable and inevitably present in all things.

C. And finally it was in order that he might become Omega that it was necessary for him, through the travail of his incarnation, to conquer and animate the universe.

Christ Is Identical with Omega

In order to demonstrate the truth of this fundamental proposition, I need only refer to the long series of Johannine — and still more Pauline — texts in which the physical supremacy of Christ over the universe is so magnificently expressed. I cannot quote them all here, but they come down to these two essential affirmations: "In eo omnia constant" (Col. 1:17), and "Ipse est qui replet omnia" (Col. 2:10, cf. Eph. 4:9), from which it follows that "Omnia in omnibus Christus" (Col. 3:11) — the very definition of Omega. I am very well aware that there are two loopholes by which timid minds hope to escape the awesome realism of these repeated statements. They may maintain that the cosmic attributes of the Pauline Christ belong to the Godhead alone; or they may try to weaken the force of the texts by supposing that the ties of dependence that make the world subject to Christ are juridical and moral, the rights exercised by a landowner, a father, or the head of an association. As regards the first subterfuge, all I need to do is to refer to the context, which is categorical: even in Col. 1:15ff, St. Paul quite obviously has in mind the theandric Christ; it was in the incarnate Christ that the universe was preformed.... It is impossible for me to read St. Paul without seeing the universal and cosmic domination of the incarnate Word emerging from his words with dazzling clarity....

The Influence of Christ-Omega

Having noted that the Pauline Christ (the great Christ of the mystics) coincides with the universal term "Omega," adumbrated by our philosophy, the grandest and most necessary attribute we can ascribe to him is that of exerting a supreme physical influence on every cosmic reality without exception....

Christ would not be the God of St. Paul, nor the God of my heart, if, looking at the lowliest, most material, created being, I were unable to say, "I cannot understand this thing, I cannot grasp it, I cannot be fully in contact with it, except as a function of him who gives to the natural whole of which it is a part its full reality and its final determined form." Since Christ is Omega, the universe is physically impregnated to the very core of its matter by the influence of his superhuman nature. The presence of the incarnate Word penetrates everything, as a universal element. It shines at the common heart of things, as a center that is infinitely intimate to them and at the same time (since it coincides with universal fulfillment) infinitely distant.

The vital, organizing influence of the universe, of which we are speaking, is essentially grace. We can see, however, from the point of view of creative union, that this wonderful reality of grace must be understood with a much greater intensity and width of meaning than is normally attributed to it. By baptism in cosmic matter and the sacramental water we are more Christ than we are ourselves — and it is precisely in virtue of this predominance in us of Christ that we can hope one day to be fully ourselves....

In reality, by virtue of Christ's establishment as head of the cosmos, they [all the processes of the universe] are steeped in final purpose, in supernatural life, even to what is most palpable in their reality. Everything around us is physically "christified," and everything, as we shall see, can become progressively more fully so.

In this "pan-Christism," it is evident, there is no false pantheism.

All around us, Christ is physically active in order to control all things. From the ultimate vibration of the atom to the loftiest mystical contemplation, from the lightest breeze that ruffles the air to the broadest currents of life and thought, he ceaselessly animates, without disturbing, all the earth's processes. And in return Christ gains physically from every one of them. Everything that is good in the universe (that is, everything that goes toward unification through effort) is gathered up by the incarnate Word as nourishment that it assimilates, transforms, and divinizes. In the consciousness of this vast two-way movement, of ascent and descent, by which the development of the *pleroma* (that is, the bringing of the universe to maturity) is being effected, believers can find astonishing illumination and strength for the direction and maintenance of their efforts. Faith in the universal Christ is inexhaustibly fruitful in the moral and mystical fields.

The Animation of the World by the Universal Christ

The concentration of the multiple in the supreme organic unity of Omega represents a most arduous task. Every element, according to its degree, shares in this laborious synthesis, but the effort called for from the upper term of unification has necessarily had to be the hardest of all. That is why the incarnation of the Word was infinitely painful and mortifying — so much so that it can be symbolized by a cross.

The first act of the incarnation, the first appearance of the cross, is marked by the plunging of the divine unity into the ultimate depths of the multiple. Nothing can enter into the universe that does not emerge from it. Nothing can be absorbed into things except through the road of matter, by ascent from plurality. For Christ to make his way into the world by any side road would be incomprehensible. The redeemer could penetrate the stuff of the cosmos, could pour himself into the life-blood of the universe, only by first dissolving himself in matter, later to be reborn from it. *Integritatem Terrae Matris non minuit, sed sacravit,* "He did not lessen, but consecrated the integrity of Mother Earth." The smallness of Christ in the cradle, and the even tinier forms that preceded his appearance among men, are more than a moral lesson in humility. They are in the first place the application of a law of birth and, following on from that, the sign of Christ's definitively taking possession of the world. It is because Christ was "inoculated" in matter that he can no longer be dissociated from the growth of spirit: that he is so ingrained in the visible world that he could henceforth be torn away from it only by rocking the foundations of the universe.

It is philosophically sound to ask of each element of the world whether its roots do not extend into the furthest limits of the past. We have much better reason to accord to Christ this mysterious preexistence. Not only *in ordine intentionis* but *in ordine naturae, omnia in eo condita sunt,* "all things are contained in him," not only "in the order of intention" but also "in the order of nature." The endless aeons that preceded the first Christmas are not empty of Christ, but impregnated by his potent influx. It is the ferment of his conception that sets the cosmic masses in motion and controls the first currents of the biosphere. It is the preparation for his birth that accelerates the progress of instinct and the full development of thought on earth.   — "My Universe" in SC 54–61

CHRIST'S HEART — UNIVERSAL CENTER OF ENERGY AND FIRE

Thanks to a sort of habit which has always been ingrained in me, I have never, at any moment of my life, experienced the least difficulty in addressing myself to God as to a supreme *Someone*. So true is this that I now understand that a certain "love of the invisible" has always been active in me, parallel to the "congenital" cosmic sense which, as we have seen, is the "backbone" of my inner life.

This appetite was a gift to me from heaven, and after it had first, working undetected, nourished my *innate* appetite for the earth it ultimately came out into the open and effected a confluence with it. And this it did through a process of *universalization,* whose first two phases may be described, as I remember them, as a "materialization," soon to be followed by an "energizing," of the notion of divine love.

To take the "materialization" of divine love first.

Biologically speaking, how could it have been otherwise in my case?

Sucked in with my mother's milk, a "supernatural" sense of the divine had flowed into me side by side with the "natural" sense of plenitude. Each of these two appetites strove to be exclusive, but neither could wipe out the other. The only conceivable result of their conflict, therefore, was an assimilation of the supernatural (the less primitive and, genetically speaking,

the more external) by the natural. And the only way in which
the assimilation could be effected was by an interior adjustment
of the divine to the evolutive: that is to say, an adjustment to
the psychological law, proper to my nature, of being unable to
worship anything except from a starting point in the tangible
and resistant.

My progress in this direction was made easier by the fact
that my "mother's God" was primarily, for me as much as
for her, the *incarnate* Word. This sufficed for the establishment
of a first contact, through the humanity of Jesus, between the
two halves of my fundamental being, the "Christian" and the
"pagan." It was precisely in that contact, however, that there
reappeared the difficulty I have already mentioned of perceiving
"the consistence of the human."

How strange and ingenuous are the reactions that take place
in the brain of a child! I can remember so well witnessing for
the first time the distressing sight of a lock of hair being burnt
up in the fire, and how my disappointment with the organic
instantaneously reacted on the very person of Christ.... If I was
to be able *fully to worship* Christ, it was essential that as a first
step I should be able to give him "solidity."

And it was at this point in the story of my spiritual life that
there emerged (and now I must beg my reader to suppress his
smile) the central, seminal, part played by the "devotion" with
which my mother constantly sustained me: devotion to the heart
of Jesus, little though she suspected the transformations that
were to be effected in it by my insatiable yearning for cosmic
organicity.

Everybody knows the historical background of the cult of the
Sacred Heart (or the love of Christ): how it was always latent
in the Church and then in the France of Louis XIV assumed
an astonishingly vigorous form, which was at the same time
oddly limited both in the object to which it was directed and
in its symbol (the heart of our Savior, depicted with curiously
anatomical realism!).

The remains of this narrow view can still, unfortunately, be seen today, both in a form of worship which is always obsessed by the idea of sin and in an iconography which we must needs deplore without too much vexation. For my own part, however, I can say that at no time has its influence held the least attraction for my piety.

For the pious person of the seventeenth century the "Sacred Heart" was, in effect, "a part" (both material and formal) of Jesus — a selected, detached, part of the Redeemer: as happens when we isolate and enlarge *some detail* of a picture in order to be able to admire it more conveniently. My own experience was quite different. The moment I saw a mysterious patch of crimson and gold delineated in the very center of the Savior's breast, I found what I was looking for — a way of finally *escaping* from everything that so distressed me in the complicated, fragile, and individual organization of the body of Jesus. It was an astounding release! ...

It would be difficult for me to convey how deeply and forcefully, and with what continuity (long before the notion of the "universal-Christ" became explicitly coherent in me) my religious life in the prewar years developed under the sign of the Heart of Jesus, *understood in this way,* and with the sense of wonder it aroused in me. At that time, the more I tried to pray, the more deeply did God "materialize" for me in a reality that was at once spiritual and tangible.

It was the immersion of the divine in the corporeal: and an inevitable reaction brought the transfiguration (or transmutation) of the corporeal into an incredible energy of radiation.

In a first stage, my mother's Christ was in some way "de-individualized" for me into a form that was "substantially" hardly representational. But then came a second stage when this humano-divine "solid" (like my earlier piece of iron and under the same psychic pressure) lit up and exploded from within. There was no longer a patch of crimson in the center of Jesus, but a glowing core of fire, whose splendor embraced every contour — first those of the God-Man — and then those of all things that lay within his ambience.

... Through and under the symbol of the "Sacred Heart," the divine had already taken on for me the form, the consistence, and the properties of an *Energy,* of a *Fire:* by that I mean that it had become able to insinuate itself everywhere, to be metamorphosed into no matter what; and so, *inasmuch as it was patient of being universalized,* it could in the future force its way into, and so amorize, the cosmic milieu in which at exactly the same moment I was ... engaged in making my home. ...

To christify matter: that sums up the whole venture of my innermost being ... a grand and glorious venture (and I still tremble often, even as I pursue it) — but I found it impossible not to hazard myself in it, so powerful was the force with which the levels of the universal and the personal came together and gradually closed up, over my head, to form one single vault.

Christ, his heart. A fire: a fire with the power to penetrate all things — and which was now gradually spreading unchecked.

At the root of this invasion and envelopment I can distinguish, I believe, the rapidly increasing importance that was being assumed in my spiritual life by the sense of "the will of God": fidelity to the divine will, by which I mean fidelity to a *directed and realized* omnipresence, which can be apprehended both actively and passively in every element of the world and in all its events. Although at first I did not precisely realize the bridge by which this eminently Christian attitude connected my love of Christ and my love of things, nevertheless I have always, ever since the first years of my religious life, gladly surrendered myself to this active feeling of communion with God through the universe. It was a decisive emergence of this "pan-Christic" mysticism, finally matured in the two great atmospheres of Asia and the war, that was reflected in 1923 and 1927 by *The Mass on the World* and *Le Milieu Divin.*   —HM 41–44, 47

VISION OF CHRIST IN THE UNIVERSE

You want to know...how the universe, in all its power and multiplicity, came to assume for me the lineaments of the face of Christ? This came about gradually; and it is difficult to find words in which to analyze life-renewing intuitions such as these; still, I can tell you about some of the experiences through which the light of this awareness gradually entered into my soul....

I was thinking: Suppose Christ should deign to appear here before me, what would he look like? How would he be dressed?...

Meanwhile my gaze had come to rest without conscious intention on a picture representing Christ offering his heart to human beings. The picture was hanging in front of me on the wall of a church into which I had gone to pray. So, pursuing my train of thought, I began to ask myself how an artist could contrive to represent the holy humanity of Jesus without imposing on his body a fixity, a too precise definition, which would seem to isolate him from all other people, and without giving to his face a too individual expression so that, while being beautiful, its beauty would be of a particular kind, excluding all other kinds.

It was, then, as I was keenly pondering over these things and looking at the picture, that my vision began. To tell the truth, I cannot say at what precise moment it began, for it had already reached a certain degree of intensity when I became conscious of it. The fact remains that as I allowed my gaze to wander over the figure's outlines I suddenly became aware that these were *melting away*: they were dissolving, but in a special manner, hard to describe in words. When I tried to hold in my gaze the outline of the figure of Christ it seemed to me to be clearly defined; but then, if I let this effort relax, at once these contours, and the folds of Christ's garment, the luster of his hair, and the bloom of his flesh, all seemed to merge as it were (though without vanishing away) into the rest of the picture. It was as though the planes which marked off the figure of Christ from the world surrounding it were melting into a single vibrant surface whereon all demarcations vanished.

It seems to me that this transformation began at one particular point on the outer edge of the figure, and that it flowed on then until it had affected its entire outline. This at least is how the process appeared to me to be taking place. From this initial moment, moreover, the metamorphosis spread rapidly until it had affected everything.

First of all I perceived that the vibrant atmosphere which surrounded Christ like an aureole was no longer confined to a narrow space about him, but radiated outward to infinity. Through this there passed from time to time what seemed like trails of phosphorescence, indicating a continuous gushing-forth to the outermost spheres of the realm of matter and delineating a sort of blood stream or nervous system running through the totality of life.

The entire universe was vibrant! And yet, when I directed my gaze to particular objects, one by one, I found them still as clearly defined as ever in their undiminished individuality.

All this movement seemed to emanate from Christ, and above all from his heart. And it was while I was attempting to trace the emanation to its source and to capture its rhythm that, as my attention returned to the portrait itself, I saw the vision mount rapidly to its climax.

I notice I have forgotten to tell you about Christ's garments. They had that luminosity we read of in the account of the transfiguration; but what struck me most of all was the fact that no weaver's hand had fashioned them — unless the hands of angels are those of nature. No coarsely spun threads composed their weft; rather it was matter, a bloom of matter, which had spontaneously woven a marvelous stuff out of the inmost depths of its substance; and it seemed as though I could see the stitches running on and on indefinitely and harmoniously blending to-

gether into a natural design which profoundly affected them in
their own nature.

But, as you will understand, I could spare only a passing
glance for this garment so marvelously woven by the continuous
cooperation of all the energies and the whole order of matter:
it was the transfigured face of the Master that drew and held
captive my entire attention.

You have often at nighttime seen how certain stars change
their color from the gleam of blood-red pearls to the luster
of violet velvet. You have seen, too, the play of colors on a
transparent bubble. So it was that on the unchanging face of
Jesus there shone, in an indescribable shimmer or iridescence,
all the radiant hues of all our modes of beauty. I cannot say
whether this took place in answer to my desires or in obedience to the good pleasure of him who knew and directed
my desires; what is certain is that these innumerable gradations of majesty, of sweetness, of irresistible appeal, following
one another or becoming transformed and melting into one another, together made up a harmony which brought me complete
satiety.

And always, beneath this moving surface, upholding it and
at the same time gathering it into a higher unity, there hovered
the incommunicable beauty of Christ himself. Yet that beauty
was something I divined rather than perceived; for whenever I
tried to pierce through the covering of inferior beauties which
hid it from me, at once other individual and fragmentary beauties rose up before me and formed another veil over the true
beauty even while kindling my desire for it and giving me a
foretaste of it.

It was the whole face that shone in this way. But the center of
the radiance and the iridescence was hidden in the transfigured
portrait's eyes.

Over the glorious depths of those eyes there passed in rain-
bow hues the reflection — unless indeed it were the creative
prototype, the idea — of everything that has power to charm

us, everything that has life.... And the luminous simplicity of the fire which flashed from them changed, as I struggled to master it, into an inexhaustible complexity wherein were gathered all the glances that have ever warmed and mirrored back a human heart. Thus, for example, these eyes which at first were so gentle and filled with pity that I thought my mother stood before me, became an instant later, like those of a woman, passionate and filled with the power to subdue, yet at the same time so imperiously pure that under their domination it would have been physically impossible for the emotions to go astray. And then they changed again, and became filled with a noble, virile majesty, similar to that which one sees in the eyes of men of great courage or refinement or strength, but incomparably more lofty to behold and more delightful to submit to.

This scintillation of diverse beauties was so complete, so captivating, and also so swift that I felt it touch and penetrate all my powers simultaneously, so that the very core of my being vibrated in response to it, sounding a unique note of expansion and happiness.

Now while I was ardently gazing deep into the pupils of Christ's eyes, which had become abysses of fiery, fascinating life, suddenly I beheld rising up from the depths of those same eyes what seemed like a cloud, blurring and blending all that variety I have been describing to you. Little by little an extraordinary expression, of great intensity, spread over the diverse shades of meaning which the divine eyes revealed, first of all permeating them and then finally absorbing them all....

And I stood dumbfounded.

For this final expression, which had dominated and gathered up into itself all the others, was *indecipherable.* I simply could not tell whether it denoted an indescribable agony or a superabundance of triumphant joy. I only know that since that moment I thought I caught a glimpse of it once again — in the glance of a dying soldier.

— "Christ in the World of Matter" in HU 39–43

GOD'S OMNIPRESENCE REVEALED
THROUGH THE PERSON OF JESUS

We have seen the mystical milieu gradually develop and assume a form at once divine and human.

At first, we might have mistaken it for a mere projection of our emotions, their excess flowing out over the world and appearing to animate it.

Soon, however, its autonomy became apparent as a strange and supremely desirable omnipresence. This universal presence began by drawing into itself all consistence and all energy....

Sometimes, when I have scrutinized the world very closely, I have thought that I could see it enveloped in an atmosphere — still very tenuous but already individualized — of mutual good will and of truths accepted in common and retained as a permanent heritage. I have seen a shadow floating, as though it were the outline of a universal soul seeking to be born.

What name can we give to this mysterious entity, who is in some small way our own handiwork, with whom, eminently, we can enter into communion, and who is some part of ourselves, yet who masters us, has need of us in order to exist, and at the same time dominates us with the full force of his absolute being?

I can feel it: he has a name and a face, but he alone can reveal his face and pronounce his name.

Jesus!

The movement that first opened my eyes began *at one point*, in a person: my own person. As my powers of perception were aroused, that point expanded as though it would absorb all things. Very soon, however, it found that the process seemed to be reversed and that it was itself being taken over. Together with all the beings around me I felt that I was caught up in a higher movement that was stirring together all the elements of the universe and grouping them in a new order. When it was given to me to see where the dazzling trail of particular beauties and partial harmonies was leading, I recognized that it was all coming to center *on a single point,* on a person, your person: Jesus!

In his superabundant unity, that person possessed the virtue of each one of the lower mystical circles. His presence impregnated and sustained all things. His power animated all energy. His mastering life ate into every other life, to assimilate it to himself. Thus, Lord, I understood that it was possible to live without ever emerging from you, without ever ceasing to be buried in you, the ocean of life, the life that penetrates and quickens us. Since first, Lord, you said, "Hoc est corpus meum," not only the bread of the altar but (to some degree) everything in the universe that nourishes the soul for the life of spirit and grace has become *yours* and has become *divine* — it is divinized, divinizing, and divinizable. Every presence makes me feel that you are near me; every touch is that touch of your hand; every necessity transmits to me a pulsation of your will. And so true is this, that everything around me that is essential and enduring has become for me the dominance and, in some way, the substance of your heart: Jesus!

That is why it is impossible for me, Lord — impossible for any person who has acquired even the smallest understanding of you — to look on your face without seeing in it the *radiance* of every reality and every goodness. In the mystery of your mystical body — your cosmic body — you sought to feel the echo of every joy and every fear that moves each single one of all the countless cells that make up humankind. And correspondingly, we cannot contemplate you and adhere to you without your Being, for all its supreme simplicity, transmuting itself as we grasp it into the restructured multitude of all that you love upon earth: Jesus!

And the result of this astonishing synthesis of all perfection and all growth that you effect in yourself is that the act by which I possess you combines, in its strict simplicity, more attitudes and more insights than I have spoken of here, and more than I could ever express. When I think of you, Lord, I cannot say whether it is in this place that I find you more, or in that place, whether you are to me friend or strength or matter, whether I am contemplating you or whether I am suffering, whether I rue my faults or find union, whether it is you I love or the whole sum of others. Every affection, every desire, every possession, every light, every depth, every harmony, and every ardor glitters with equal brilliance, at one and the same time, in the inexpressible *relationship* that is being set up between me and you: Jesus!

— "The Mystical Milieu" in WTW 144–47

PRAYERS TO THE EVER-GREATER CHRIST

Lord Jesus, now that beneath those world-forces you have become truly and physically everything for me, everything about me, everything within me, I shall gather into a single prayer both my delight in what I have and my thirst for what I lack; and following the lead of your great servant I shall repeat those inflamed words in which, I firmly believe, the Christianity of tomorrow will find its increasingly clear portrayal:

> Lord, lock me up in the deepest depths of your heart; and then, holding me there, burn me, purify me, set me on fire, sublimate me, till I become utterly what you would have me be, through the utter annihilation of my ego. . . .

As long as I could see — or dared to see — in you, Lord Jesus only the man who lived two thousand years ago, the sublime moral teacher, the friend, the brother, my love remained timid and constrained. Friends, brothers, wise men: have we not many of these around us, great souls, chosen souls, and much closer to us? And then can man ever give himself utterly to a nature which is purely human? Always from the very first it was the world, greater than all the elements which make up the world, that I was in love with; and never before was there anyone before whom I could in honesty bow down. And so for a long time, even though I believed, I strayed, not knowing what it was I loved. But now, Master, today, when through the manifestation of those superhuman powers with which your resurrection endowed you, you shine forth from within all the forces of the earth and so become visible to me, now I recognize you as my sovereign, and with delight I surrender myself to you.

How strange, my God, are the processes your spirit initiates! When, two centuries ago, your Church began to feel the particular power of your heart, it might have seemed that what was captivating people's souls was the fact of their finding in you an element even more determinate, more circumscribed, than your humanity as a whole. But now on the contrary a swift reversal is making us aware that your main purpose in this revealing to us of your heart was to enable our love to escape from the constrictions of the too narrow, too precise, too limited image of you which we had fashioned for ourselves. What I discern in your breast is simply a furnace of fire; and the more I fix my gaze on its ardency the more it seems to me that all around it the contours of your body melt away and become enlarged beyond all measure, till the only features I can distinguish in you are those of the face of a world which has burst into flame.

Glorious Lord Christ: the divine influence secretly diffused and active in the depths of matter, and the dazzling center where all the innumerable fibers of the multiple meet; power as implacable as the world and as warm as life; you whose forehead is of the whiteness of snow, whose eyes are of fire, and whose feet are brighter than molten gold; you whose hands imprison the stars; you who are the first and the last, the living and the dead and the risen again; you who gather into your exuberant unity every beauty, every affinity, every energy, every mode of existence; it is you to whom my being cried out with a desire as vast as the universe, "In truth you are my Lord and my God." ...

For me, my God, all joy and all achievements, the very purpose of my being and all my love of life, all depend on this one basic vision of the union between yourself and the universe. Let others, fulfilling a function more august than mine, proclaim your splendors as pure spirit; as for me, dominated as I am by a vocation which springs from the inmost fibers of my being, I have no desire, I have no ability, to proclaim anything except the innumerable prolongations of your incarnate being in the world of matter; I can preach only the mystery of your flesh, you the soul shining forth through all that surrounds us.

It is to your body in this its fullest extension — that is, to the world become through your power and my faith the glorious living crucible in which everything melts away in order to be born anew; it is to this that I dedicate myself with all the resources which your creative magnetism has brought forth in me: with the all too feeble resources of my scientific knowledge, with my religious vows, with my priesthood, and (most dear to me) with my deepest human convictions. It is in this dedication, Lord Jesus, I desire to live, in this I desire to die.

— "The Mass on the World" in HM 130–34

•

Because, Lord, by every innate impulse and through all the hazards of my life I have been driven ceaselessly to search for you and to set you in the heart of the universe of matter, I shall have the joy, when death comes, of closing my eyes amid the splendor of a universal transparency aglow with fire....

It is as if the fact of bringing together and connecting the two poles, tangible and intangible, external and internal, of the world which bears us onward had caused everything to burst into flames and set everything free....

And all this took place because, in a universe which was disclosing itself to me as structurally convergent, you, by right of your resurrection, had assumed the dominating position of all-inclusive center in which everything is gathered together.

A fantastic molecular swarm which — either falling like snow from the inmost recesses of the infinitely diffuse, or on the other hand surging up like smoke from the explosion of some infinitely simple — an awe-inspiring multitude, indeed, which whirls us around in its tornado! ... It is in this terrifying granular energy that you, Lord — so that I may be able the better to touch you, or rather (who knows?) to be more closely embraced by you — have clothed yourself for me: nay, it is of this that you have formed your very body. And for many years I saw in it no more than a wonderful contact with an already completed perfection....

Until that day, and it was only yesterday, when you made me realize that when you espoused matter it was not merely its immensity and its organicity that you had taken on: what you did was to absorb, concentrate, and make entirely your own its unfathomable reserves of spiritual energies.

So true is this that ever since that time you have become for my mind and heart much more than he who was and who is; you have become *he who shall be....*

Yet can anything, Lord, in fact do more for my understanding and my soul to make you an object of love, the only object of love, than to see that you — the center ever opened into your own deepest core — continue to grow in intensity, that there is an added glow to your luster, at the same pace *as you pleromize yourself* by gathering together the universe and subjecting it ever more fully at the heart of your being ("until the time for returning, you and the world in you, to the bosom of him from whom you came")?

The more the years go by, Lord, the more I believe that I can see that in myself and in the world around me the most important though unvoiced concern of modern man is much less a struggle for the possession of the world than a search for a way of escaping from it. The agony of feeling that one is imprisoned in the cosmic bubble, not so much spatially as ontologically! The fretful hunt for a way out for evolution — or, more exactly, for its point of focus! In the modern world, that is the sorrow, the price to be paid for a growing planetary reflection, that lies heavy, but as yet hardly recognized, on the soul of both Christian and gentile.

As humankind emerges into consciousness of the movement that carries it along, it has a continually more urgent need of a direction and a solution ahead and above, to which it will at last be able to consecrate itself.

Who, then is this God, no longer the God of the old cosmos but the God of the new cosmogenesis — so constituted precisely because the effect of a mystical operation that has been going on for two thousand years has been to disclose in you, beneath the child of Bethlehem and the crucified, the moving principle and the all-embracing nucleus of the world itself? Who is this God for whom our generation looks so eagerly? Who but you, Jesus, who represents him and brings him to us?

Lord of consistence and union, you whose *distinguishing mark* and *essence* is the power indefinitely to grow greater, without distortion or loss of continuity, to the measure of the mysterious matter whose heart you fill and all whose movements you ultimately control, Lord of my childhood and Lord of my last days, God, complete in relation to yourself and yet, for us, continually being born, God, who, because you offer yourself to our worship as "evolver" and "evolving," are henceforth the only being that can satisfy us, sweep away at last the clouds that still hide you, the clouds of hostile prejudice and those, too, of false creeds.

Let your universal presence spring forth in a blaze that is at once diaphany and fire.

O ever-greater Christ!

— "The Heart of Matter" in HM 55–58

THE CHRISTIFIED UNIVERSE

Christian tradition is unanimous that there is more in the total Christ than man and God. There is also he who, in his "theandric" being, gathers up the whole of creation: *in quo omnia constant.*

Hitherto, and in spite of the dominant position accorded to it by St. Paul in his view of the world, this third aspect or function — we might even say, in a true sense of the words, this third "nature" of Christ (neither human nor divine, but cosmic) — has not noticeably attracted the explicit attention of the faithful or of theologians.

Things have changed today: we now see how the universe, along all the lines known to us experientially, is beginning to grow to fantastic dimensions, so that the time has come for Christianity to develop a precise consciousness of all the hopes stimulated by the dogma of the universality of Christ when it is enlarged to this new scale, and of all the difficulties, too, that it raises.

Hopes, of course: because, if the world is becoming so dauntingly vast and powerful, it must follow that Christ is very much greater even than we used to think. But difficulties, too: because, in a word, how can we conceive that Christ "is immensified" to meet the demands of our new space-time, without thereby losing his personality — that side of him that calls for our worship — and without in some way evaporating?

It is precisely here that in a flash there comes into the picture the astounding, emancipating, harmony between a religion that is christic and an evolution that is convergent in type.

Were the world a static cosmos — or if, again, it formed a divergent system — the only relations we could invoke as a basis for Christ's primacy over creation would be (make no mistake about this), by nature, conceptual and juridical. He would be Christ the king of all things because he has been *proclaimed* to be such — and not because any organic relationship of dependence exists (or could even conceivably exist) between him and a multiplicity that is fundamentally *irreducible.*

From such an "extrinsical" point of view, one could hardly, with any honesty, speak of a christic "cosmicity."

But if, on the other hand, and as the facts make certain, the universe — our universe — does indeed form a sort of biological "vortex" dynamically centered upon itself, then we cannot fail to see the emergence at the system's temporo-spatial peak, of a unique and unparalleled position, where Christ, effortlessly and without distortion, becomes literally and with unprecedented realism, the *Pantocrator.*

Starting from an evolutive Omega at which we assume Christ to stand, not only does it become possible to conceive Christ as radiating *physically* over the terrifying totality of things but, what is more, that radiation must inevitably work up to a maximum of penetrative and activating power.

Once he has been raised to the position of prime mover of the evolutive movement of complexity-consciousness, the cosmic Christ becomes cosmically possible. And at the same time, *ipso facto,* he acquires and develops in complete plenitude a veritable *omnipresence of transformation.* For each one of us, every energy and everything that happens are superanimated by his influence and his magnetic power. To sum up, cosmogenesis reveals itself, along the line of its main axis, first as biogenesis and then noogenesis and finally culminates in the Christogenesis which every Christian venerates.

And then there appears to the dazzled eyes of the believer the eucharistic mystery itself, extended infinitely into a veritable universal transubstantiation in which the words of the consecration are applied not only to the sacrificial bread and wine but, mark you, to the whole mass of joys and sufferings produced by the convergence of the world as it progresses.

And it is then, too, that there follow in consequence the possibilities of a universal communion.

Hitherto human beings had tried only two roads in their efforts to unite themselves to the divine. The first was to escape from the world into "beyond." The second, on the other hand, was to allow themselves to dissolve into things and to be united with them monistically. What else, in fact, could human beings try in a cosmic economy if they wished to escape from the internal and external multiplicity that was tormenting them?

By contrast, from the moment when the universe, through cosmogenesis directed upon a christic Omega, assumes for us the shape of a truly convergent whole, a third and completely new road opens up by which the "mystic" may arrive at total unity. And (since the whole sphere of the world is precisely a center in process of centration upon itself) that road is to give all one's strength and all one's heart to coinciding with the focus of universal unification, as yet diffuse but nevertheless already in existence.

With the christified universe (or, which comes to the same thing, with the universalized Christ) an evolutive supermilieu appears — which I have called "the divine milieu" — and it is now essential that every human being should fully understand the specific properties (or "charter") of that milieu, which are themselves linked with the emergence of completely new psychic dimensions.

All that I have just been saying leads up to this, that what basically characterizes the divine milieu is that it constitutes a dynamic reality in which all opposition between universal and personal is being wiped out, but not by any confusion of the two: the multiple "reflected" elements of the world attaining their fulfillment, each one still within its own infinitesimal *ego*, by integrant accession to the christic *Ego....*

God can in the future be experienced and apprehended (and can even, in a true sense, be completed) by the whole ambient totality of what we call evolution — *in Christo Jesu....*

This is still, of course, Christianity and always will be, but a

Christianity reincarnated for the second time (Christianity, we might say, squared) in the spiritual energies of matter.

— "The Christic" in HM 93–96

UNIVERSAL COMMUNION

I am beginning to understand: under the sacramental species it is primarily through the "accidents" of matter that you touch me, but, as a consequence, it is also through the whole universe in proportion as this ebbs and flows over me under your primary influence. In a true sense the arms and the heart which you open to me are nothing less than all the united powers of the world which, penetrated and permeated to their depths by your will, your tastes, and your temperament, converge upon my being to form it, nourish it, and bear it along toward the center of your fire. In the host it is my life that you are offering me, O Jesus.

What can I do to gather up and answer that universal and enveloping embrace? To the total offer that is made me, I can only answer by a total acceptance. I shall therefore react to the eucharistic contact with the entire effort of my life — of my life of today and of my life of tomorrow, of my personal life and of my life as linked to all other lives. Periodically, the sacred species may perhaps fade away in me. But each time they will leave me a little more deeply engulfed in the layers of your omnipresence: living and dying, I shall never at any moment cease to move forward in you. Thus the precept implicit in your Church, that we must communicate everywhere and always, is justified with extraordinary force and precision. The eucharist must invade my life. My life must become, as a result of the sacrament, an unlimited and endless contact with you, that life which seemed, a few moments ago, like a baptism with you in the waters of the world, now reveals itself to me as communion with you through

the world. It is the sacrament of life. The sacrament of my life —
of my life received, of my life lived, of my life surrendered....

Because you ascended into heaven after having descended
into hell, you have so filled the universe in every direction,
Jesus, that henceforth it is blessedly impossible for us to escape
you.... Now I know that for certain. Neither life, whose advance increases your hold upon me, nor death, which throws
me into your hands, nor the good or evil spiritual powers,
which are your living instruments, nor the energies of matter
into which you have plunged, nor the irreversible stream of duration whose rhythm and flow you control without appeal, nor
the unfathomable abysses of space which are the measure of
your greatness,... none of these things will be able to separate
me from your substantial love, because they are all only the veil,
the "species," under which you take hold of me in order that I
may take hold of you....

Once again, Lord, I ask which is the most precious of these
two beatitudes: that all things for me should be a contact with
you? Or that you should be so "universal" that I can undergo
you and grasp you in every creature?

Sometimes people think that they can increase your attraction in my eyes by stressing almost exclusively the charm and
goodness of your human life in the past. But truly, O Lord, if I
wanted to cherish only a man, then I would surely turn to those
whom you have given me in the allurement of their present
flowering. Are there not, with our mothers, brothers, friends,
and sisters, enough irresistibly lovable people around us? Why
should we turn to Judaea two thousand years ago? No, what
I cry out for, like every being, with my whole life and all my
earthly passion, is something very different from an equal to
cherish: it is a God to adore.

To adore... that means to lose oneself in the unfathomable,
to plunge into the inexhaustible, to find peace in the incorruptible, to be absorbed in defined immensity, to offer oneself to the
fire and the transparency, to annihilate oneself in proportion as

one becomes more deliberately conscious of oneself, and to give of one's deepest to that whose depth has no end. Whom, then, can we adore?...

Disperse, O Jesus, the clouds with your lightning! Show yourself to us as the Mighty, the Radiant, the Risen! Come to us once again as the Pantocrator who filled the solitude of the cupolas in the ancient basilicas! Nothing less than this parousia is needed to counterbalance and dominate in our hearts the glory of the world that is coming into view. And so that we should triumph over the world with you, come to us clothed in the glory of the world. —MD 116–18

Chapter 4

The Awakening and Growth of the Spirit in the World

Faith consecrates the world.
— MD 130

For Teilhard, God's creative action takes place through the immense evolutionary process in the universe. Human beings are an integral part of this process, shaped and molded by universal energies, but in turn they themselves also contribute and help to shape the direction of this process. Human efforts assist in building up the body of God, the divine kingdom. The struggles of the universe reach into the most hidden parts of our being so that, given the power to see, we can recognize God's action through all events and things in our lives. Thus life becomes for the believer one long act of living communion with the incarnate Word and with God's creative action.

As Teilhard understood evolution as an increasing process of spiritualization, he was particularly interested in the awakening and rise of the spirit in the world. This involves a fundamental change in human awareness and consciousness, and the nurturing of a spirituality that feeds and strengthens the taste and zest for life. For this, physical, mental, and spiritual energies are needed. The earth is in a state of growth where we can witness the birth of spiritual realities among much turmoil and tension.

Teilhard compares the "building of the earth" to the tending of a garden with numerous plants and diverse soil, or to the construction of a house with many materials brought by different laborers. At a deeper level, he understands the awakening and growth of the spirit from a religious and mystical perspective as an increase in the reality and consistence of the incarnate Word becoming flesh in the world.

Numerous are the passages where these ideas are mentioned or developed at some length. From his long experience as a researcher and traveler mixing with different social groups and creeds, Teilhard was acutely aware that the modern ideal of the divine and the nature of human religiousness were undergoing radical changes. Contemporary spiritual sensibility is closely linked to the scientific understanding of life in the universe, to the importance of human efforts, to the responsibility for our environment and planet. The most sincere and passionate human aspirations must thus be integrally linked with our understanding of God. Yet Christians often fail to comprehend and respond to the desires and anxieties of the earth. The Church needs to link the Gospel of Christ to the gospel of human effort so that its message is presented in a way that relates to people's experience and feelings. It is not enough to encourage Christians "to feel with the Church"; the Church as a true mother must in turn be able "to feel with the people." This is what Teilhard wrote in his "Note on the Presentation of the Gospel in a New Age," drafted just after the end of the First World War, in January 1919. The first text selected below is taken from that essay. More than most, Teilhard was early aware that we are standing at the threshold of a new era, living in a new kind of society, globally interlinked, with our former geocentric, anthropocentric, and Eurocentric illusions being replaced by a new vision of the world. Few perceived this radical shift in human consciousness so acutely and so early in the twentieth century.

Teilhard also believed that the fundamentally psychic and

*spiritual nature of evolution is linked to a rise in inwardness
and the growth of the spirit. He realized that inner energies
were needed for human evolution to move forward and upward, toward a higher plane. He was always concerned with
feeding the zest for living, for building the earth, for developing a planetary society with more equality, peace, and justice
for all. To maintain the taste for life and feed the zest for living
can never simply be taken for granted, just as we cannot take
our health as a simple given but have to examine, cultivate, and
take care of it. Zest for life is especially needed at the current
stage when evolution has become conscious of itself in the self-
reflective experience of human beings. An ardent taste for life is
required not only to maintain the dynamics of life and ensure its
continuity on earth, but also to answer our psychological need
of what we are living for, what our goals are. Human beings
need to define their goals — otherwise they will have neither energy nor zest, but will go on strike because they will get bored
with life and drop out from taking responsibility for it. This real
danger, so much more obvious today, may in fact be the greatest
obstacle on the path to further human development.*

*Teilhard was always passionately concerned with this theme
of feeding the zest, the ardor of life within the human community. He even dreamed of founding an institute of human
energetics in order to study in a systematic, scientific manner
this decisive question of how to provide the necessary spiritual
energies for coping with life. Of all the forms of human energy by far the strongest is the power to love, which more than
anything else can help us to come together and create bonds
through loving union and communion.*

*One of the finest visions of his dream of a united human
community is found in the essay "The Spirit of the Earth"
(1931), from which the third passage below is taken. This essay celebrates God as spiritual and personal center of cosmic
evolution, the ultimate goal and center of the immense universal stream of becoming and of all human striving. It also*

praises the dynamics of human unification, initially most visible in the numerous material links now increasingly being forged between different groups and societies around the globe. This material network is in advance of what Teilhard calls the "soul-making" that is needed to create a stronger community among the human family. Such bonds, however, cannot be created nor strengthened without the participation of the different world religions, for they possess an ocean of energy reserves able to help solve the problems of human action. Teilhard perceived a planetary need for a faith to deal with the present crisis in the world which is essentially a spiritual crisis for him, just as it was for Carl Gustav Jung. What interested Teilhard most were the spiritual energy reserves found in the still active currents of faith in the world today. What can the world faiths contribute to the solution of contemporary problems such as unemployment or war? What ethical insights do they possess to guide human action? What vision of God do they convey to draw us to higher spiritual ideals?

Such were some of the questions he reflected upon in "The Zest for Living" (1950), one of the talks he gave, together with some others, to an interfaith group in post–Second World War Paris. In a quiet but sustained way Teilhard was a great supporter of ecumenical and interfaith ideas* while always emphasizing the transformative power of the Christian faith, its action-oriented and activating potential due to its incarnational rootedness in the world. This power of spiritual transformation is celebrated in many of his writings; it is visible in his approach to the spiritual significance of suffering, or the experience of true happiness, in his reflections on the energies of sexual attraction and embodied love, or in his description of the feminine as an element of union.

---

*For a more detailed discussion of Teilhard's understanding of the spiritual contribution of world faiths see my book *Christ in All Things: Exploring Spirituality with Teilhard de Chardin* (Maryknoll, N.Y.: Orbis Books, 1997), chapter 6, "Interfaith Dialogue and Christian Spirituality."

Teilhard celebrated the powers of love, love in the cosmos, love between woman and man, love between different members of the human family. He saw love and union as central to Christianity. The Christian God is above all a God of love who can ultimately only be reached through love. Teilhard dreamed of a humanity that forms one single body animated by one single heart. A great visionary of human unity, he ultimately saw the building of the human community as a spiritual task leading human hearts to the heart of God, a heart burning like a blaze of fire in the midst of matter and radiating energy through the entire universe, consecrated and made holy by the powers of love and creative union.

THE SUMMONS OF THE SPIRIT WITHIN HUMAN ASPIRATIONS

The great converters, or perverters, of men have always been those in whom the soul of their age burnt the most intensely.

We have in our day, . . . a *natural* religious movement of great force.

We Christians, do we realize that if we are to influence it and supernaturalize it (and that is what is really meant by the conversion of the world) it is essential that we share — *non verbo tantum, sed re* — in its drive, in its anxieties and its hopes?

So long as we appear to wish to impose on the people of today a ready-made divinity from outside, then, surrounded by the multitude though we may be, we shall inevitably be preaching in the desert.

There is only one way of enthroning God as sovereign over people of our time: and that is to embrace the ideal they reach out to; it is to *seek, with them,* the God whom we already possess but who is as yet *among us* as though he were a stranger to us.

Who is the God whom our contemporaries seek, and how can we succeed in *finding him, with them,* in Jesus? ...

The deep-rooted religious movement of our age seems to me to be characterized by the appearance (in human consciousness) of the *universe* — seen as a *natural* whole, *more noble* than humans — and *therefore equivalent,* for people, *to a God* (finite or infinite).

The features of this God are still indistinct. It is not so much his brilliance we see as that of the aureole that surrounds him, in that quarter where lie life, truth, and spirit. But his radiance is beyond all doubt.

A more exact view of things — replacing a certain illusion (geo-, anthropo-centric) — is showing us today our own being lost in such a reservoir of energies and mysteries, our own individuality subject to so many ties and extensions of itself, our civilization surrounded by so many other cycles of thought, that the feeling of the crushing dominance of the world over us as persons is being impressed upon everyone who shares in the vision of their own time....

Next, although modern people cannot yet give an exact name to the great Being who is being embodied *for them* and *through them* in the world, they already know that they will never worship a divinity unless it possesses *certain attributes* by which they will be able to recognize it.

The God for whom our century is waiting must be:

1. as *vast* and mysterious as the cosmos,

2. as *immediate* and all-embracing as life,

3. as *linked* (in some way) *to our effort* as is humanity.

A God *who made the World less mysterious, or smaller, or less important to us, than our heart and reason show it to be,* that God — *less beautiful than the God we await* — *will never again be the one before whom the world will kneel.*

Of this we must be quite clear: the *Christian ideal* (as normally expressed) has ceased to be what we still complacently flatter ourselves that it is, the common ideal of humanity.

More and more people, if they wish to be sincere, will have to admit that Christianity seems to them to be inevitably *inhuman* and *inferior,* both in its promises of individual happiness and in its precepts of renunciation. "Your Gospel," they are already saying, "leads to the formation of souls that *have an interest in* their own selfish advantages — *with no interest* in the common task; and so it has *no interest* for us. Our concept is better than that: and therefore there is more truth in ours."

The precedence assumed, in modern consciousness, by the whole over the individual is rapidly tending to produce a new *moral ideal,* in which justice ranks higher than charity, work higher than detachment, whole-hearted effort to develop higher than mortification.

"Christian" and "human" are tending no longer to coincide. In that lies the great schism that threatens the Church.

Let no one declare that this schism is imaginary — or at all events that the blame lies entirely with those who are going their own way.

Life, as a whole, makes no mistakes. And where is life to be found today? Can we really say that it is to be found with us? . . .

And what, above all, is the summons of the spirit within us? . . .

The special apostolate I urge — which aims at sanctifying not simply a nation or a social category, but *the very axis of the human drive toward spirit* — includes two distinct phases: the first, and natural, phase providing an introduction to the Christian faith, and the second, supernatural, phase showing (in the light of revelation) how far and in what direction earthly activity can be carried.

1. In a first introductory phase, I believe that we must develop — in those who believe in Jesus Christ just as much as in unbelievers — a *fuller consciousness of the universe* that encompasses us and of our capacity to influence its development by our action.

This religious, mystical passion, smoldering in us, this passion for the natural whole of which we form a part, must (to judge from my own case) be nourished and systematized: as much to vitalize the religion of the faithful believers as to pave the way for the faith-adherence of unbelievers....

As for the others, those who already possess the dominating intuition of the universal, I am convinced that we cannot do more useful work for the kingdom of God than by encouraging and confirming them in their vision.

Going beyond the limited and precarious associations effected among nations — the alliances, the large economic or scientific unions — I believe that it is the part of the Christian ... to raise people to the idea of *some human effort,* unique and specific, which would bring together all activities: no longer merely in the defensive (as we saw at times during the war) but in the positive pursuit of a supreme ideal — an ideal that cannot fail to reach exact definition through our patient and convergent efforts toward a larger measure of truth, of beauty, and of justice.

To present to people the brilliance (which fits in with what they have today a presentiment of) and *to share with them* the hope of some crowning glory for the universe — and, in order to do this, to neglect nothing when it is a question of associating them in the unity of one single terrestrial faith: such, to my mind, should be the human, preparatory, form of our zeal and our preaching.

And, working in this field, we Christians would be fully associated with the most noble and most vital section of our contemporaries, whatever their religious convictions.

— "Notes on the Presentation of the Gospel
in a New Age" in HM 210–15

FEEDING THE ZEST FOR LIFE
WITHIN HUMANITY

By "zest for living" or "zest for life," I mean here, to put it very approximately, that spiritual disposition, at once intellectual and effective, in virtue of which life, the world, and action seem to us, on the whole, luminous — interesting — appetizing. . . .

It is something utterly and entirely different from a mere emotional state.

At first sight, the presence in each one of us of this "rock-bottom will" and its degree of intensity might seem to have importance and value only as affecting *individual* well-being; one would be inclined to say that it was a private health problem — something to be discussed in each case with one's doctor.

However, if we examine it more thoroughly, we shall find that the importance of the problem it raises is of a very different nature.

In the reflections that follow, I hope to make it clear that in the "zest for life" there is

- nothing less than the *energy of universal evolution,* which, in the form of an innate pull toward being, wells up in what is most primitive, and therefore the least directly controllable, in each one of us;

- an energy, *the feeling and development* of which is to some degree *our responsibility;*

- and this we must do by a supremely vital *operation,* the most sensitive part of which is *entrusted* to the expert knowledge and skill of *religions.* . . .

In the world all around us, an immense variety of fathomless currents spread wide and run together in a way that might at first seem impossible to understand.

Gradually, however, under long and intensive observation, an order and a hierarchy emerge in the end from this confused muddle. . . .

To what type of energy known to us is it possible ultimately to attribute the sort of preference accorded by nature in her experimenting to the more complex (and in consequence more "psychized') combinations that emerge from the cosmic play of large numbers — a preference she shows in spite of their extreme fragility?

Since Darwin there has been much talk (and with justification) of "the survival of the fittest." Yet surely it is obvious that if this Darwinian struggle is to be effective it inevitably *presupposes* in the competing elements a *tenacious sense of conservation,* of survival — in which we meet again in a concentrated form the very essence of the whole mystery. . . .

A zest for living, *the zest* for living — such, when we get to the bottom of the problem, would appear to be the fundamental driving force which impels and directs the universe along its main axis of complexity-consciousness. . . .

If what I have just been saying about the fundamentally psychic nature of evolution is correct, it is immediately apparent that a new and hitherto strangely neglected element is unexpectedly introduced into the various calculations by which our science is at this moment trying to construct an energetics of the human mass. . . .

Imagine (and in the eyes of our existentialists this is no chimera) that, by extending our power of vision, we have become capable of reaching the confines of our cosmic domain and sees tomorrow that we are decisively caught in the trap of a blind universe, cold and hermetically sealed. Is it not obvious that in this case anthropogenesis — while it is true that it might for some time drag along from force of habit or inclination — would be struck to the heart as though by a plight, so that before long its actual leading shoot would wither away?

It is, in truth, a strange prospect and one which for a very long time now I have been unable to dismiss from my mind: that all over the earth the attention of thousands of engineers and economists is concentrated on the problem of world resources of coal, oil, or uranium — and yet nobody, on the other hand, bothers to carry out a survey of the zest for life: to take its "temperature," to feed it, to look after it, and (why not, indeed?) to increase it.

Like a sick person revolted by the sight of a banquet, so human beings, struck down by biological nausea, would certainly go on strike against life — even though they had reached the zenith of their power to discover and create. And this strike will certainly *come about* unless, keeping pace with science and power, there is an upsurge in human beings of an ever more impassioned interest in the task entrusted to them. In us, evolution (in Julian Huxley's phrase) has become conscious, dangerously and critically so — conscious and perfected to the point of being able to control its own driving forces and to rebound upon itself. But what good would this great cosmic event be to us if we were *to lose the zest for evolution?*

We still treat this precious and primordial appetite just as healthy people do their health — as though it were a fixed, assured, capital: the world, we imagine, will always have plenty of it available for us.

A most dangerous sense of security, and a more grave error in dynamics!

In the end, the ultra-human cannot be built except with the human; and the human is, essentially, nothing but a will to subsist and grow greater, which can equally well be intensified or wither away.

It is, then, to the theoretical and practical study of this will (a will that radically conditions all our forms of power) that a new science — the most important, perhaps, of all sciences — must be devoted: and tomorrow it will inevitably be so devoted. Its problem will be, "How to maintain deep in the heart of human bcings the source of their vital impulse and open it up ever more widely."

A priori, we dispose of two very different, and at the same time allied, methods of tackling the problem so presented.

a. We may either, acting physico-chemically on the "complexity" focus of our being, try, by the application of certain substances or certain methods, permanently to increase our organic vitality. And we all know, do we not, the passing moods of intense excitement (or on the other hand, of depression) which follow upon such treatments.

b. Or, acting psychically on the "consciousness" focus, we may work intellectually and affectively to release and heighten in ourselves, and provide a solid basis for, ever more powerful rational motives and inducements for living. . . .

Which of these two methods should we choose?

It is obviously impossible completely to separate the two, since once again we find in them the mysterious interaction of body and spirit. On the other hand, at the point in evolution at which the earth stands at this moment, it is difficult not to accord a large measure of priority (not only in dignity, but also in effectiveness and urgency) to the effort to cultivate in people today an increasing reflective passion for the universe which envelops them — or, more precisely, for the cosmogenesis which is engendering them.

In a world which has become conscious of its own self and provides its own motive force, what is most vitally necessary to the thinking earth is a faith — and a great faith — and ever more faith.

To know that we are not prisoners.

To know that there is a way out, that there is air, and light, and love, somewhere, beyond the reach of all death.

To know this, to know that it is neither an illusion nor a fairy story.

That, if we are not to perish smothered in the very stuff of our being, is what we must at all costs secure.

And it is there that we find what I may well be so bold as to call the *evolutionary role* of religions.

— "The Zest for Living" in AE 231–38

GOD AS SPIRITUAL AND PERSONAL CENTER OF COSMIC EVOLUTION

Let us now return to the earth itself and try to guess what the further periods of its spiritual evolution will be.

In the course of a first phase, one may legitimately suppose that the narrow limits to which it confines us, far from being a cause of weakness, represent on the contrary a necessary condition of progress. There is, as we have already pointed out, a spirit of the earth. But in order to take form and shape, this spirit needs a powerful concentrating agent to bring people together and increase their powers of acting as a crowd. We can already see before our eyes the first coming together of the human layer taking place in the form of an interpenetration of thoughts and interests. No similar effect would be possible in an inhabited field without limits. Let us extend, in thought, this process of continuous unification, in the course of which the inner affinities of the elements are forced together by the very form of the planet on which we dwell. What new power may not issue from this drastic treatment of "spiritual matter"? It pains us to be thus forced into a mold, since our liberties are momentarily hampered and because, certain material links being (perhaps inevitably) *in advance* in this task of "soul-making," we feel ourselves to be coming to the state of the machine and the termite colony. But let us put our trust in spiritual energies. True union does not stifle or confuse its elements; it super-differentiates them in unity. A little more time and the spirit of the earth will emerge from this ordeal with its specific individuality, its own character and features. And then, on the surface of the noosphere, gradually elevated in its preoccupations and passions — always reaching out to solve higher problems and possess greater objects — *the striving for being will reach its maximum....*

Contemporary humanity has passed through a period of great illusion in imagining that, having attained a better knowledge of itself and the world, it has no more need of religion. The result of the two great modern discoveries of space and time, culminating in the knowledge of evolution, has undoubtedly been to produce many detailed schematizations. It may consequently have seemed (at least for a moment) that nothing of our past beliefs remained. Indeed there have been a great number of systems in which the fact of religion was interpreted as a psychological phenomenon linked with the childhood of humanity. At its greatest, at the origins of civilization, it had gradually to decline and give place to more positive theories from which God (a personal and transcendent God above all) must be excluded. This was a pure illusion. In reality, for anyone who can see, the great conflict from which we have just emerged has merely strengthened the world's need for belief. Having reached a higher stage in self-mastery, the spirit of the earth is discovering a more and more vital need to worship; *from universal evolution God emerges* in our minds greater and more necessary than ever.

Let us briefly sketch, now that we are able to understand them a little better, the great phases of this continuous arising of God (looking below the veil and details of the great religions).

The birth and progress of the idea of God on earth are intimately bound up with the phenomenon of hominization. At the very moment when life reflects on itself — by virtue of that same movement — it finds itself facing *the problem of action*. It becomes awake to itself on the ascending and difficult road of progressive unification. How will it explain to itself this primal and congenital duty? Where will it find not only the authority but the courage and desire for this effort?...No consideration should, rightly speaking, persuade us to take a single step forward without a knowledge that the ascending path leads to *a peak from which life will never descend again*. The sole possible instigator of reflective life must therefore be an absolute, that is to say a divine goal. Religion can become an opium. It is too often understood as a simple soothing of our woes. *Its true function is to sustain and spur on the progress of life*. We are far from wishing to imply that from its beginnings this conviction stood out in the human mind as clearly as it does for us today. But we can recognize now that, underlying much simpler and more childish interpretations, there was really this profound need for an absolute. Beneath all the progressive forms of religion, it is the absolute that was sought.

Now once we have established this point of departure, it becomes clear that the "religious function," born of hominization and linked with it, cannot but grow continuously with the human itself. . . . Is not this a fact that we can observe all around us? At what moment has there been a more urgent need in the noosphere to find a faith and hope in order to give sense and a soul to the immense organism we are constructing? Has the struggle ever been more violent between love and hatred of life? We really waver today between two desires: to serve the world or to go on strike. Since life cannot possibly perish or, therefore, revolt against itself, we must be very close to the open triumph of adoration!

And indeed, step by step with the growing expectation of humanity, the face of God seems gradually to loom larger through the world. God has sometimes seemed to disappear, eclipsed by the organic vastness of the cosmos that was being revealed to us. Once we understand that the universe is supported solely by the future and the spirit, these new immensities cannot fail to reveal to us the majesty, the grandeur, and the overpowering richness of the summit toward which all things converge. The "unbelievers" of our time bow willingly before "energy-as-god." But it is impossible to stop at this somewhat vague stage of materialist pantheism. Under penalty of being less evolved than the ends brought about by its own action, *universal energy must be a thinking energy.* Consequently, as we shall see, the attributes of cosmic value, with which it is irradiated to our modern eyes, in no way abolish our need to recognize it as a transcendent *form of personality.*

The personality of God (together with the survival of the "soul") calls out the greatest opposition and antipathy from contemporary scientific thought. The origin of this dislike is to be found in the intellectual contempt which has rejected as "anthropocentric" all attempts to understand the universe through the human. Let us once more put the fact of the human in its true place. Let us recognize, not out of vanity or idleness but on scientific evidence that no phenomenon has had more preparation or is more axial and characteristic than this. And at the same time we are compelled to admit that even (and particularly) today, because of the new value the human being is assuming in nature, the idea of a God conceived as a distinct and animate center of the world is necessarily in full growth. Let us say, in fact, substituting one equivalent formula for another, that by the capital event of *hominization,* the most advanced portion of the cosmos has become *personalized.* This simple change of variable brings in sight, for the future, a double condition of existence which is quite inevitable.

First of all, since everything *in the universe beyond the human* takes place within *personalized being,* the final divine endpoint of universal convergence must also (eminently) possess the quality of a person (without which it would be inferior to the elements it governs)....

We have followed the cosmic spiritual phenomenon *from within* by the path of simple immanence. But now by logic of this path itself, we are forced to turn and to recognize that the current which elevates matter must be conceived rather as a *tide* than as a simple internal pressure. Multiplicity ascends attracted and engulfed by something which is "already one." This is the secret and guarantee of the irreversibility of life.

In an initial phase — before the human being — the attraction was vitally but blindly received by the world. Since the arrival of humans, it has become at least partially conscious in the form of reflective freedom, and it has given rise to religion. Religion is not a strictly individual crisis — or choice or intuition — but represents the long disclosure of God's being through the collective experience of the whole of humanity: God reflecting himself personally on the organized sum of thinking monads to guarantee an assured success and fix precise laws for their hesitant activities; God bent over the now intelligent mirror of earth to impress on it the first marks of his beauty.

The last phase of this vast revelation, whose history is one with that of the world, cannot be other than the history of union, which will take place when the attraction of God, victorious over the material resistances caused by unorganized plurality, will once and for all have rescued from inferior determinism the spirit slowly nourished by all the sap of the earth.

How will the spiritual evolution of our planet end? . . . Perhaps, we will now say, in a psychic rather than material turning about — possibly like a death — which will in fact be liberation from the material plane of history and ecstasy in God.

— "The Spirit of the Earth" in HE 42–47

THE ROLE OF RELIGIONS
WITHIN THE DEVELOPMENT OF THE WORLD

The idea came to be widely accepted during the nineteenth century that religions express a primitive state of humankind that has now been left behind. "In former times men developed the concept of divinity in their imagination in order to account for natural phenomena of whose causes they were ignorant. By discovering the empirical explanation of these same phenomena, science has made God and religions superfluous." That sums up the new creed of many of our contemporaries.

It is of the utmost importance to react against this narrow way of understanding the origin and the history of the idea of God in the world. There can be no doubt that the old forms assumed by religious sentiment were, to a great extent, confused. For a long time religion permeated, with no distinction of plane, a complex psychological mass from which there have in turn emerged experimental science, history, civic life, and so on, all with their own special methods and results. But this is a long way from meaning that the need for the absolute (on which all religions are based) disappeared in the course of that differentiation. As we shall see, we have only to look at the world of today, and more particularly the crisis it is now going through, with an impartial mind (we might even say a positivist mind) to be convinced of the contrary. Like a bud from which the scales have fallen, the religious nucleus in which all that is best in the life-sap of human beings is concentrated can be seen at this very moment emerging more distinct and vigorous than ever.

If we are to understand the origin, development, and present state of the religious question, we must, at least provisionally, ignore all secondary considerations of methods of worship and interpretation and look squarely at the biological revolution produced in the terrestrial world by the appearance of the human being, that is, of thought. Before the human being, the whole of vital energy was almost entirely absorbed at every moment by the work of obtaining food, of reproduction, and of morphological evolution: the animals, like overworked laborers, had not a moment's respite from their immediate task. They had neither the time nor the interior power to raise their heads and reflect. In humans, on the contrary (as though the drill had suddenly struck oil), an overflow of power suddenly gushed to the surface. Because of their psychological organization, human beings constantly (both in the space they cover and the time they foresee) exceed the work required by their animality. Through the human being, an ocean of free energy (an energy as real and as "cosmic" as the others with which physics is concerned) sets out to cover the earth....

The function, then, of religion, which is so often contemptuously relegated to metaphysics, is precisely in its turn to provide a foundation for morality by introducing a dominating principle of order and an axis of movement into the restless and undisciplined multitude of reflective atoms: something of supreme value, to create, to hold in awe, or to love.

Religion, therefore, was not developed primarily as an easy way out, to provide shelter from the insoluble or intrusive difficulties met by the mind as it became active. In its real basis, it is biologically (we might almost say mechanically) the necessary counterpart to the release of the earth's spiritual energy: the human being, by his appearance in nature, brings with him the emergence, ahead of him, of a divine pole to give him balance, just as necessarily as, in the particulate world explored by physics, the positive and negative elements of matter are linked together.

If that is so, the phenomenon of religion cannot be regarded as the manifestation of a transitory state, which is destined to grow weaker and disappear with the growth of humankind. The release of energy effected in the terrestrial system by the establishment of the human zoological type constantly increases with the passage of time, so giving us a definition of and a standard of measurement for whatever reality is hidden under the word "progress." Through his social organization, which apportions and divides the common task, human beings constantly increase the proportion of independence and leisure available to every citizen. By the introduction of machinery they suddenly increase this superabundance to a formidable degree. The whole human economy (once it fully understands its "planetary" role) can have no other goal than constantly to enlarge on earth the excess of the psychic over matter. And that can mean only one thing: that religion, born to animate and control this overflow of spirit, must itself grow greater and more clearly defined in step with it and in the same degree. As soon as there is a gap between the release of conscious energy and the intensification of the sense of religion, then disorder is introduced; and it is all the more dangerous in that the human being is more adult. Is it not precisely this that we are now witnessing?

"Lack of employment": This phrase defines, in its most immediately apparent and most tangible aspect, the crisis the world is passing through at this moment: but at the same time it expresses the underlying cause of the evil that distresses us. Humankind began to be without occupation (at least potentially) from the first moment when its newborn mind was released from perception and immediate action to wander in the domain of things that are distant or possible. But it did not have a profound sense of being without occupation (in fact, but even more in logic) so long as a predominant part of itself was still enslaved to a task that absorbed the greater part of its capacity for work. There are many symptoms to indicate that it is now without occupation and that it may well continue to become increasingly so, now that the balance has finally been upset between material needs and powers of production, so that, in theory, all people have to do is to allow the machine that emancipated them to run on, and fold their arms. The present crisis is much more than a difficult interval accidentally encountered by a particular type of civilization. Under contingent and local appearances, it expresses the inevitable result of the loss of equilibrium brought about in animal life by the appearance of thought. People no longer know today how to occupy their physical powers: but what is more serious, they do not know toward what universal and final end they should direct the driving force of their souls. It has already been said, though without sufficiently deep appreciation of the words: the present crisis is a spiritual crisis.

— "Christianity in the World" in SC 98–101

•

The world is being converted spontaneously to a sort of natural religion of the universe, which is wrongly turning it away
from the God of the Gospel: it is in this that its "unbelief" consists. We must convert that conversion itself, taking it one step
further, by showing, through our whole lives, that only Christ,
in quo omnia constant, is capable of animating and guiding the
newly sensed progress of the universe: and from the very extension of what is producing today's unbelief, there will perhaps
emerge the faith of tomorrow.

— "Modern Unbelief" in SC 117

•

With the rise of modern technology and thought it was not
difficult to believe ... that we had left behind the age, or phase,
of religions. It is quite certain, too, that in the light of science —
recast in its crucible — a profound refashioning and a dynamic
sorting out have been effected in the field of "creeds" and "beliefs." Nevertheless we are beginning to realize that this is far
from meaning that where mysticism is concerned the flames
of experimental knowledge have been exclusively destructive.
On the contrary ... forces of religion are emerging from the ordeal they have just gone through as a more important auxiliary
to human phylogenesis than ever before: this is because it is
henceforth to them, as "nursemaids of our faith," that we must
look for the maintenance and development of the energy required for the newly recognized needs of a vigorously active
anthropogenesis: to give enthusiasm for growth — *the zest for
the world.*

In our day, this is something that can never be emphasized
too forcibly. Because, as we are coming to see for ourselves,
the universe is organically resting on — cantilevered on, I might
say — the future as its sole support, precisely in view of that,
and because of that, the "reserves of faith" (that is, the quantity
and quality of the religious sense available) must continually
increase in our world.

Moreover, in consequence of this, we must add that the era (I do not say of *religions*) but of *religion* has by no means been left behind: it is quite certainly only beginning....

We are surrounded by a certain sort of pessimists who continually tell us that our world is foundering in atheism. But should we not rather say that what it is suffering from is *unsatisfied theism*? People, you say, no longer want God; but are you quite sure that what they are rejecting is not simply the image of a God who is too insignificant to nourish in us this concern to survive and super-live to which the need to worship may ultimately be reduced?

Hitherto the various creeds still commonly accepted have been primarily concerned to provide every person with an *individual* line of escape; this is because they were born and grew up in a time when problems of cosmic totalization and maturing *did not exist*. However universal their promises and visions of the beyond might be, they did not explicitly (and with good reason) allow any room to a global and controlled transformation of the whole of life and thought in their entirety. And yet, in the light of what we have already seen, is it not precisely an event of this order (an event that involves the expectation and the advent of some ultrahuman) that we are asking them to include, to hallow, and to animate, now and forever after?

No longer simply a religion of individuals and of heaven, but a religion of humankind and the earth — that is what we are looking for at this moment, as the oxygen without which we cannot breathe.

In these circumstances, we are forced to recognize that nothing can subsist tomorrow — nothing has any chance of heading (as must be done) the general movement of planetary hominization — except those mystical currents which are able, through a synthesis of the traditional faith in the above and our generation's newborn faith in some issue toward the ahead, to make ready and provide a complete pabulum for our "need to be."

A sifting and general convergence of religions, governed by and based on their value as an evolutionary stimulus — that, in short, is the great phenomenon of which we would appear to be at this moment both the agents and the witnesses.

But, then, it will be said, if the great spiritual concern of our times is indeed a realignment and readjustment of old beliefs toward a new Godhead who has risen up at the anticipated pole of cosmic evolution, then why not simply slough off the old — why not, that is, regroup the whole of the earth's religious power directly and *a novo* upon some "evolutionary sense" or "sense of the human" — and pay no attention to the ancient creeds? If we wish to satisfy the planetary need for faith and hope which is continually increasing with the world's technico-social organization, why not have a completely fresh faith rather than a rejuvenation and confluence of "old loves"?

Why not? For two good reasons, is my answer: they have both a solid foundation in nature, and they may be set out as follows.

First of all, there can be no doubt that, in each of the great religious branches that cover the world at this moment, a certain spiritual attitude and vision which have been produced by centuries of experience are preserved and continued; these are as indispensable and irreplaceable for the integrity of a total terrestrial religious consciousness as the various "racial" components which have successively been produced by the phylogenesis of our living group may well be for the looked-for perfecting of a final human zoological type. In the matter of religion, just as in that of cerebration, the cosmic forces of complexification, it would seem, proceed not through individuals but through complete branches.

This, however, is not all. What is carried along by the various currents of faith that are still active on the earth, working in their incommunicable core, is no longer only the irreplaceable elements of a certain complete image of the universe. Very much more even than *fragments of vision,* it is *experiences of contact* with a supreme Inexpressible which they preserve and pass on. . . .

Beneath its apparent naïveté, this is an extraordinarily daring outlook; and, if it is justified, its effect is profoundly to recast the whole theory of the zest for life and its maintenance in the world.

To preserve and increase on earth that "pressure of evolution" it is vitally important, I pointed out, that through the mutual buttressing provided by the reflection of religious ideas a progressively more real and more magnetic God be seen by us to stand out at the higher pole of hominization. We now find another condition of cosmic animation and another possibility in it. It is that, sustained and guided by the tradition of the great human mystical systems along the road of contemplation and prayer, we succeed in entering directly into receptive communication with the very source of all interior drive.

The vital charge of the world, maintained not simply by physiological artifices or by rational discovery of some objective or ideal, bringing with it — but poured directly into the depths of our being, in its higher, immediate, and most heightened form — love, as an effect of "grace" and "revelation."

The zest for life: the central and favored ligament, indeed, in which can be seen, within the economy of a supremely organic universe, a supremely intimate bond between mysticism, research, and biology.

— "The Zest for Living" in AE 238–42

THE TRANSFORMATIVE POWER OF CHRISTIAN FAITH

Faith, as we understand it . . . is not, of course, simply the intellectual adherence to Christian dogma. It is taken in a much richer sense to mean belief in God charged with all the trust in his beneficent strength that the knowledge of the divine Being arouses in us. It means the practical conviction that the universe, between the hands of the Creator, still continues to be the clay in which he shapes innumerable possibilities according to his will....

Domine, adjuva incredulitatem meam. *Ah, you know it yourself, Lord, through having borne the anguish of it as man: on certain days the world seems a terrifying thing: huge, blind, and brutal. It buffets us about, drags us along, and kills us with complete indifference. Heroically, it may truly be said, the human being has contrived to create a more or less habitable zone of light and warmth in the midst of the great, cold, black waters — a zone where people have eyes to see, hands to help, and hearts to love. But how precarious that habitation is! At any moment the vast and horrible thing may break in through the cracks — the thing which we try hard to forget is always there, separated from us by a flimsy partition: fire, pestilence, storms, earthquakes, or the unleashing of dark moral forces — these callously sweep away in one moment what we had laboriously built up and beautified with all our intelligence and all our love.*

Since my dignity as a man, O God, forbids me to close my eyes to this — like an animal or a child — that I may not succumb to the temptation to curse the universe and him who made it, teach me to adore it by seeing you concealed within it. O Lord, repeat to me the great liberating words, the words which at once reveal and operate: Hoc est corpus meum....

We have only to believe. And the more threatening and irreducible reality appears, the more firmly and desperately must we believe. Then, little by little, we shall see the universal horror unbend, and then smile upon us, and then take us in its more than human arms.

No, it is not the rigid determinism of matter and of large numbers, but the subtle combinations of the spirit that give the universe its consistency. The immense hazard and the immense blindness of the world are only an illusion to him who believes. *Fides, substantia rerum.*

Because we have believed intensely and with a pure heart in the world, the world will open the arms of God to us. It is for us to throw ourselves into these arms so that the divine milieu should close around our lives like a circle. That gesture of ours will be one of an active response to our daily task. *Faith consecrates the world.*   —MD 126, 128–30

TRANSFORMING SUFFERING
INTO SPIRITUAL ENERGY

If a perfectly keen-eyed observer were to watch the earth for a long time from a great height, our planet would first of all appear to him blue from the oxygen that envelops it; then green from the vegetation which covers it; then luminous — and ever more luminous — from the thought that grows in intensity on its surface; but at the same time it would appear dark — and ever more dark — from a suffering that, throughout the ages, grows in quantity and poignancy in step with the rise of consciousness.

Consider the total suffering of the whole earth at every moment. If only we were able to gather up this formidable magnitude, to gauge its volume, to weigh, count, analyze it — what an astronomic mass, what a terrifying total! And from physical torture to moral agonies, how subtle a range of shades of misery! And if only, too, through the medium of some conductivity suddenly established between bodies and souls, all the pain were mixed with all the joy of the world, who can say on which side the balance would settle, on that of pain or that of joy?

Yes, the more the human being becomes human, the more

deeply ingrained and the more serious — in his flesh, in his nerves, in his mind — becomes the problem of evil: evil that has to be understood and evil that has to be borne.

A sounder view of the universe in which we are caught up, it is true, is now providing us with the beginning of an answer to this problem. We are realizing that within the vast process of arrangement from which life emerges, every success is necessarily paid for by a large percentage of failures. One cannot progress in being without paying a mysterious tribute of tears, blood, and sin. It is hardly surprising, then, if all around us some shadows grow more dense at the same time as the light grows brighter: for, when we see it from this angle, suffering in all its forms and all its degrees is (at least to some extent) no more than a natural consequence of the movement by which we were brought into being.

Bowing to the evidence of a universal experience, we are beginning in an abstract way, in our minds, to admit this complementary mechanism of good and evil; but if our hearts are to conform without rebelling to this harsh law of creation, is it not psychologically necessary that we discover, in addition, some positive value in this painful wastage attaching to the operation which forms us, a value that will transfigure it and make it permanently acceptable?

Of that there can be no doubt. And it is here that there comes in to play its irreplaceable part, the astounding Christian revelation of a suffering which (provided it be accepted *in the right spirit*) can be transformed into an expression of love and a principle of union: suffering that is first treated as an enemy who has to be defeated; then suffering vigorously fought against to the bitter end; and yet at the same time suffering rationally accepted and cordially welcomed inasmuch as by forcing us out of our egocentrism and compensating for our errors it can supercenter us upon God. Yes, indeed: suffering in obscurity, suffering with all its repulsiveness, elevated for the humblest of patients into a supremely active principle of universal humanization and divinization — such is seen to be at its peak the fantastic spiritual dynamic force, born of the cross.

— "The Spiritual Energy of Suffering" in AE 247–48

•

Illness naturally tends to give sufferers the feeling that they are useless or even a burden on the earth. Almost inevitably they feel as if cast up by the great stream of life, lying by sheer ill luck incapable of work or activity. Their state seems to have no meaning. It reduces them, they might say, to inaction amid a universe in action. . . .

What a vast ocean of human suffering spreads over the entire earth at every moment! Of what is this mass formed? Of blackness, gaps, and rejections? No, let me repeat, of potential energy. In suffering the ascending force of the world is concealed in a very intense form. The whole question is how to liberate it and give it a consciousness of its significance and potentialities. The world would leap high toward God if all the sick together were to turn their pain into a common desire that the kingdom of God should come to rapid fruition through the conquest and organization of the earth. All the sufferers of the earth joining their sufferings so that the world's pain might become a great and unique act of consciousness, elevation, and union. Would not this be one of the highest forms that the mysterious work of creation could take in our sight?

Could it not be precisely for this that the creation was completed in Christian eyes by the passion of Jesus? We are perhaps in danger of seeing on the cross only an individual suffering, a single act of expiation. The creative power of that death escapes us. Let us take a broader glance, and we shall see that the cross is the symbol and place of an action whose intensity is beyond expression. Even from the earthly point of view, the crucified Jesus, fully understood, is not rejected or conquered. It is on the contrary he who bears the weight and draws ever higher toward God the universal march of progress. Let us act like him, in order to be in our whole existence united with him.

— "The Significance and Positive Value of Suffering" in HE 48, 51–52

FINDING HAPPINESS THROUGH BEING CENTERED

The only true happiness is...the happiness of growth and movement.

Do we want to be happy, as the world is happy, and with the world? Then we must let the tired and the pessimists lag behind. We must let the hedonists take their homely ease, lounging on the grassy slope, while we ourselves boldly join the group of those who are ready to dare the climb to the topmost peak. Press on!

Even so, to have chosen the climb is not enough. We have still to make sure of the right path. To get up on our feet ready for the start is well enough. But, if we are to have a successful and enjoyable climb, which is the best route?

...Life in the world continually rises toward greater consciousness, proportionate to greater complexity — as though the increasing complexity of organisms had the effect of deepening the center of their being....

When we examine the process of our inner unification, that is to say, of our personalization, we can distinguish three allied and successive stages, or steps, or movements. If a human being is to be fully himself and fully living, he must, (1) be centered upon himself; (2) be "decentered" upon "the other"; (3) be super-centered upon a being greater than himself.

We must define and explain in turn these three forward movements, with which (since happiness, we have decided, is an effect of growth) three forms of attaining happiness must correspond.

1. First, *centration*. Not only physically, but intellectually and morally too, human being are human only if they cultivate themselves — and that does not mean simply up to the age of twenty.... If we are to be fully ourselves we must therefore work all our lives at our organic development: by which I mean that we must constantly introduce more order and more unity into our ideas, our feelings, and our behavior. In this lies the whole program of action, and the whole value and meaning (all the hard work, too!) of our interior life, with its inevitable drive toward things that are ever increasingly spiritual and elevated. During this first phase each one of us has to take up again and repeat, working on his own account, the general labor of life. Being is in the first place making and finding one's own self.

2. Secondly, *decentration*. An elementary temptation or illusion lies in wait for the reflective center which each one of us nurses deep inside. It is present from the very birth of that center, and it consists in fancying that in order to grow greater each of us should withdraw into the isolation of our own self, and egoistically pursue in ourselves alone the work, peculiar to us, of our own fulfillment: that we must cut ourselves off from others, or translate everything into terms of ourselves. However, there is not just one single human being on the earth. That there are, on the contrary, and necessarily must be, myriads and myriads at the same time is only too obvious. And yet, when we look at that fact in the general context of physics, it takes on a cardinal importance — for it means, quite simply, this: that, however individualized by nature thinking beings may be, each person still represents no more than an atom, or (if you prefer the phrase) a very large molecule; in common with all the other similar molecules, he forms a definite corpuscular system from which he cannot escape. Physically and biologically the human being, like everything else that exists in nature, is essentially plural. The human is correctly described as a "mass phenomenon." This means that, broadly speaking, we cannot reach our own

ultimate without emerging from ourselves by uniting ourselves with others, in such a way as to develop through this union an added measure of consciousness — a process which conforms to the great law of complexity. Hence the insistence, the deep surge, of love, which, in all its forms, drives us to associate our individual center with other chosen and specially favored centers: Love, whose essential function and charm are that it completes us.

3. Finally, *super-centration*. Although this is less obvious, it is absolutely necessary to understand it.

If we are to be fully ourselves, as I was saying, we find that we are obliged to enlarge the base on which our being rests; in other words, we have to add to ourselves something of "the other." Once a small number of centers of affection have been initiated...this expansive movement knows no check. Imperceptibly, and by degrees, it draws us into circles of ever-increasing radius. This is particularly noticeable in the world of today. From the very beginning, no doubt, the human being has been conscious of belonging to one single great humanity. It is only, however, for our modern generations that this indistinct social sense is beginning to take on its full and real meaning. Throughout the last ten millennia (which is the period which has brought the sudden speeding up of civilization) people have surrendered themselves, with but little reflection, to the multiple forces (more profound than any war) which were gradually bringing them into closer contacts with one another; but now our eyes are opening, and we are beginning to see two things. The first is that the closed surface of the earth is a constricting and inelastic mold, within which, under the pressure of an ever-increasing population and the tightening of economic links, we human beings are already forming but one single body. And the second thing is that through the gradual building-up within that body of a uniform and universal system of industry and science our thoughts are tending more and more to function like the cells of one and the same brain. This must inevitably mean that as the transformation follows its natural line of progress we can foresee the time when human beings will understand what it is, animated by one single heart, to be united together in wanting, hoping for, and loving the same things at the same time.

The humanity of tomorrow is emerging from the mists of the future, and we can actually see it taking shape: a "super-humanity," much more conscious, much more powerful, and much more unanimous than our own. And at the same time... we can detect an underlying but deeply rooted feeling that if we are to reach the ultimate of our own selves, we must do more than link our own being with a handful of other beings selected from the thousands that surround us: we must form one whole with all simultaneously.

We can draw but one conclusion from this twofold phenomenon which operates both outside ourselves and inside ourselves: that what life ultimately calls upon us to do in order that we may be is to incorporate ourselves into and to subordinate ourselves to an organic totality of which, cosmically speaking, we are no more than conscious particles. Awaiting us is a center of a higher order — and already we can distinguish it — not simply beside us, but *beyond* and *above* us.

We must, then, do more than develop our own selves, more than give ourselves to another who is our equal, we must surrender and attach our lives to one who is greater than ourselves.

In other words: first, be. Secondly, love. Finally, worship.

Such are the natural phases of our personalization.

These, you must understand, are three linked steps in life's upward progress; and they are in consequence three super-imposed stages of happiness — if, as we have agreed, happiness is indissolubly associated with the deliberate act of climbing.

The happiness of growing greater, of loving, or of worshiping.   — "Reflections on Happiness" in TF 116–20

THE ENERGIES OF LOVE
AND SEXUAL ATTRACTION

Love is the most universal, the most tremendous, and the most mysterious of the cosmic forces. After centuries of tentative effort, social institutions have externally diked and canalized it. Taking advantage of this situation, the moralists have tried to submit it to rules. But in constructing their theories they have never got beyond the level of an elementary empiricism influenced by out-of-date conceptions of matter and the relics of old taboos. Socially, in science, business, and public affairs, men pretend not to know it, though under the surface it is everywhere. Huge, ubiquitous, and always unsubdued — this wild force seems to have defeated all hopes of understanding and governing it. It is therefore allowed to run everywhere beneath our civilization. We are conscious of it, but all we ask of it is to amuse us, or not to harm us. Is it truly possible for humanity to continue to live and grow without asking itself how much truth and energy it is losing by neglecting its incredible power of love?

From the standpoint of spiritual evolution, which we here assume, it seems that we can give a name and value to this strange energy of love. Can we not say quite simply that in its essence it is the attraction exercised on each unit of consciousness by the center of the universe in course of taking shape? It calls us to the great union, the realization of which is the only process at present taking place in nature. By this hypothesis, according to which (in agreement with the findings of psychological analysis) love is the primal and universal psychic energy, does not everything become clear around us, both for our minds and our actions? We may try to reconstruct the history of the world from outside by observing the play of atomic, molecular, or cellular combinations in their various processes. We may attempt, still more efficaciously, this same task from within by following the progress made by conscious spontaneity and noting the successive stages achieved. The most telling and profound way of describing the evolution of the universe would undoubtedly be to trace the evolution of love.

In its most primitive forms, when life was scarcely individualized, love is hard to distinguish from molecular forces; one might think of it as a matter of chemisms or tactisms. Then little by little it becomes distinct, though still *confused* for a very long time with the simple function of reproduction. Not till hominization does it at last reveal the secret and manifold virtues of its violence. "Hominized" love is distinct from all other love, because the "spectrum" of its warm and penetrating light is marvelously enriched. No longer only a unique and periodic attraction for purposes of material fertility, but an unbounded and continuous possibility of contact between minds rather than bodies; the play of countless subtle antennae seeking one another in the light and darkness of the soul; the pull toward mutual sensibility and completion, in which preoccupation with preserving the species gradually dissolves in the greater intoxication of two people creating a world.

—"The Spirit of the Earth" in HE 32–34

•

The energy which fuels our interior life and determines its fabric is in its primitive roots of a passionate nature. Like every other animal, the human being is essentially a tendency toward union that brings mutual completion, a capacity for loving, as Plato said long ago. It is from this primordial impulse that the luxuriant complexity of intellectual and emotional life develops and becomes more intense and diverse. For all their height and the breadth of their span, our spiritual ramifications have their roots deep in the corporeal. It is from the human storehouse of passion that the warmth and light of the soul arise, transfigured. It is there, initially, that we hold concentrated, as in a seed, the finest essence, the most delicately adjusted spring, governing all spiritual development.

When we have finally weighed things up, it is apparent that only spirit is worth our pursuit; but deep within us there exists a system of linkages, both sensitive and profound, between spirit and matter. It is not only that the one, as the Christian moralists say, supports the other: it is *born* of the other....

The Christian code of virtue seems to be based on the presupposition that woman is for man essentially an instrument of generation. Either woman exists for the propagation of the race — or woman has no place at all: such is the dilemma put forward by the moralists. All that is most dear to us in our experiences, and most certain, revolts against this simplification. However fundamental woman's maternity may be, it is almost nothing in comparison with her spiritual fertility. Woman brings fullness of being, sensibility, and self-revelation to the man who has loved her. The truth is as old as man himself; but it could not take on its full value until the world had reached such a degree of psychological consciousness that, for a human race that had spread far and wide and had a sound economic footing, the problems of food supplies and of reproduction had begun to be dominated by those of maintaining and developing spiritual energies. In fact, making the widest allowance for the phenomena of moral retrogression and license, it would appear that the present "freedom" of morals has its true cause in the search for a form of union which will be richer and more spiritualizing than that which is limited to the cradle. Here we have a symptom, which may be interpreted as follows.

Within the human mass there floats a certain power of development, represented by the forces of love, which infinitely surpasses the power absorbed in the necessary concern for the reproduction of the species. The old doctrine of chastity assumed that this drive could and should be diverted directly toward God, with no need of support from the creature. In this there was a failure to see that such an energy, still largely potential (as are all the other spiritual powers of matter), also required a long period of development in its natural plane. In the present state of the world, man has not yet, in reality, been completely revealed to himself by woman, nor is the reciprocal revelation complete. In view, therefore, of the evolutive structure of the universe, it is impossible for one to be separated from the other while their development is still continuing. It is not in isolation (whether married or unmarried), but in paired units, that the two portions, masculine and feminine, of nature are to rise up toward God. The view has been put forward that there can be no sexes in spirit. This arises from not having understood that their duality was to be found again in the composition of divinized being. . . .

There is a general question of the feminine, and so far it has been left unresolved or imperfectly expressed by the Christian theory of sanctity. It is this that accounts for our dissatisfaction with, and our repugnance to, the old discipline of virtue. It used to be urged that the natural manifestations of love should be reduced as much as possible. We now see that the real problem is how to capture and transform the energies they represent. We must not cut them down, but go beyond them. Such will be our new ideal of chastity. . . .

Hitherto, asceticism has been a pressure toward rejection; the chief requirement of holiness used to be self-deprivation. In the future, because of our new moral outlook on matter, spiritual detachment will be something much more like a conquest; it will mean plunging into the flood of created energies, in order both to be uplifted and to uplift them — and *this includes* the first and most fiery of those energies. Chastity (just as resignation, "poverty," and the other evangelical virtues) is essentially *a spirit.* And so we can begin to see the outline of a general solution to the problem of the feminine.

In itself, *detachment by passing through* is in perfect harmony with the idea of the incarnation, in which Christianity is summed up. The movement carried out by the man who plunges into the world, in order first to share in things and then to carry them along with him — this movement, let me emphasize, is an exact replica of the baptismal act: "He who descended," says St. Paul, "is he also who ascended...that he might fill all things."...This comparatively new proposition, that Christian perfection consists not so much in purifying oneself from the refuse of the earth as in divinizing creation, is a forward step. In the most conservative quarters, it is beginning to be recognized that there is a communion with God through earth—a sacrament of the world—spreading like a halo round the eucharist; but there is still a grudging reserve in allotting the share that has at last been accorded to terrestrial sources of nourishment. As in the biblical Eden, the majority of fruits are now allowed to the initiate. His, if he feels their attraction, the "vocation," his the joys of artistic creation, the conquests of thought, the emotional excitement of discovery. These broadenings of personality are accepted as sanctifying or sanctifiable. One tree, however, still carries the initial prohibition, the tree of the feminine. And so we are still faced by the same dilemma—either we can have woman only in marriage, or we must run away from the feminine.

Why this exception ? Why this departure from logic?...

In practice, the feminine is included among natural products that are forbidden as being too dangerous: a disturbing scent, an intoxicating draught. Since the beginning of time, men have been astounded by the uncontrollable power of this element; and in the end, being unable to suppress its use entirely, our mentors have come to limit it to essential cases. There is no distrust (though logically there might well be, perhaps) of the passions for ideas or numbers, or even of a keen interest in stars or nature. Because these realities are assumed (quite wrongly) to appeal only to reason, they are regarded as harmless and easily spiritualized. Sexual attraction, on the contrary, is frightening because of the complex and obscure forces it may at any moment bring into operation. Love, it would seem, is a monster slumbering in the depths of our being, and throughout our lives, we can be safe from it only if we are careful not to disturb its sleep.

I am far from denying the destructive and disintegrating forces of passion. I will go so far as to agree that apart from the reproductive function, men have hitherto used love, on the whole, as an instrument of self-corruption and intoxication. But what do these excesses prove? Because fire consumes and electricity can kill, are we to stop using them? The feminine is the most formidable of the forces of matter. True enough. "Very well, then," say the moralists, "we must avoid it." "Not at all," I reply, "we take hold of it." In every domain of the real (physical, affective, intellectual) *"danger" is a sign of power....* Avoiding the risk of a transgression has become more important to us than carrying a difficult position for God. And it is this that is killing us. "The more dangerous a thing, the more is its conquest ordained by life": it is from that conviction that the modern world has emerged; and from that our religion, too, must be reborn....

I have reached the point where I believe I can distinguish, as I look around me, the two following phases in the creative transformation of human love. During a first phase of humanity, man and woman are confined to the physical act of giving and the concern with reproduction; and around that fundamental act they gradually develop a growing nimbus of spiritual exchanges. At first it was no more than an imperceptible fringe, but the fruitfulness and mystery of union gradually find their way into it; and it is on the side of that nimbus that the balance ultimately comes to rest. However, at that very moment, the center of physical union from which the light emanated is seen to be incapable of accepting further expansion. The center of attraction suddenly withdraws ahead, to infinity, we might say; and, in order to continue to possess one another more fully in spirit, the lovers are obliged to turn away from the body, and so seek one another in God. Virginity rests upon chastity as thought upon life: through a reversal of direction, or at one particular point of coincidence.

Such a transformation on the face of the earth cannot, of course, be instantaneous. Time is essentially necessary. When you heat water, the whole quantity does not turn into steam at the same moment: the liquid phase and the gaseous phase exist together for a long time. Nor could it be otherwise. Nevertheless, one single event is taking place beneath this duality — and its significance and "worth-whileness" extend to the whole. So, at this present moment, physical union retains its necessity and its importance for the race; but its spiritual quality is henceforth defined by the type of higher union it first makes possible and then sustains. Love is going through a "change of state" in the noosphere; and, if what all the great religions teach us is correct, it is in this new direction that humanity's collective passage to God is being mapped out.

It is in this form that I picture to myself the evolution of chastity.

Theoretically, this transformation of love is quite possible. All that is needed to effect it is that the pull of the *personal* divine center be felt with sufficient force to dominate the natural attraction that would tend to cause the pairs of human monads to rush prematurely into one another's arms.

In practice, I am forced to admit, the difficulty of this enterprise seems so great that 90 percent of my readers would say that all I have written here is overingenuous or even wildly absurd. Surely universal experience has shown conclusively that spiritual loves have always ended in grossness? The human being is made to walk with feet on the ground. Has anyone ever had the idea of flying?

Yes, I shall answer: some mad people have had such a dream; and that is why we have today conquered the skies. What paralyzes life is lack of faith and lack of audacity. The difficulty lies not in solving problems but in identifying them. And so we cannot avoid this conclusion: it is biologically evident that to gain control of passion and so make it serve spirit must be a condition of progress. Sooner or later, then, the world will brush aside our incredulity and take this step: because whatever is the more true comes out into the open, and whatever is better is ultimately realized.

The day will come when, after harnessing the ether, the winds, the tides, gravitation, we shall harness for God the energies of love. And, on that day, for the second time in the history of the world, human beings will have discovered fire.

— "The Evolution of Chastity"
in TF 68, 70–75, 85–87

LOVE AND UNION
AS CENTRAL TO CHRISTIANITY

"Love one another." Those words were pronounced two thousand years ago. But today they sound again in our ears in a very different tone. For centuries charity and fraternity could only be presented as a code of moral perfection, or perhaps as a practical method of diminishing the pains or frictions of earthly life. Now since the existence of the noosphere, on the one hand, and the vital necessity we are under of preserving it, on the other, have been revealed to our minds, the voice which speaks takes on a more imperious tone. It no longer says only: "Love one another in order to be perfect," but adds, "Love one another or you perish." "Realistic" minds are welcome to smile at dreamers who speak of a humanity cemented and armored no longer with brutality but with love. They are welcome to deny that a maximum of physical power may coincide with a maximum of gentleness, and goodness. Their critical scepticism cannot prevent the theory and experience of spiritual energy from combining to warn us that *we have reached a decisive point in human evolution,* at which the only way forward is in the direction of a common passion, a "conspiration."

To go on putting our hopes in a social order obtained by external violence would simply mean to abandon all hope of carrying the spirit of the earth to its limits.

Now human energy, being the expression of a movement as irresistible and infallible as the universe itself, cannot possibly be prevented by any obstacle from freely reaching the natural goal of its evolution.

Therefore, despite all checks and all improbabilities, we are inevitably approaching a new age, in which the world will throw off its chains and at last give itself up to the power of its inner affinities.

Either we must doubt the value of everything around us, or we must utterly believe in the possibility, and I should now add in the inevitable consequences, of universal love....

Let us try ... to sketch in broad outline the human history of universal love.

Central to the process leading to the recent establishment of an affective relationship of a personal order between the human being and the universe, we must inevitably place the influence of Christianity (whether we believe or not in its transcendent value).

The phenomenon of Christianity seems to me to have been obscured by the way in which people have often tried to define it by certain characteristics which are only accidental or secondary to it. Simply to present the teaching of Christ as an awakening of the human being to his personal dignity or as a code of purity, gentleness and resignation, or again as the starting point of our Western civilization, is to mask its importance and make its success incomprehensible by ignoring its characteristically new content. The essential message of Christ, I should say, is not to be sought in the Sermon on the Mount, nor even in the drama of the cross; it lies wholly in the proclamation of a "divine fatherhood" or, to translate, in the affirmation that God, a personal being, presents himself to us as the goal of a personal *union*. Many times already (and especially at the dawn of the Christian era) the religious groping of humanity had drawn near to this idea that God, a spirit, could only be reached by spirit. But it is in Christianity alone that the movement achieves its definitive expression and content. The gift of the heart in place of the prostration of the body; communion beyond sacrifice; God as love, and only to be finally reached in love; this is the psychological revolution, and the secret of the triumph of Christianity. Now since this initial illumination the flame has never ceased to grow....

Just as the eye of the natural scientist (if he or she decides to seek the true constant of evolution in the growth of consciousness) discovers the thrust of a continually mounting stem among the accidental thicket of living species, so historians of religions, once they decide to measure the march of Christianity not only by the numerical expansion of the faithful but by the *qualitative evolution of an act of love* find themselves tracing the curve of an undoubted progress.

Now let us understand a further point. The growth of the human collective consciousness at present taking place does not prevent there having been in the world before us (in a *not too* distant past) people better endowed as individuals than many of our contemporaries, nor would I affirm that the love of God did not have in Paul, Augustine, or Teresa of Avila a certain potential richness that we should have difficulty in finding in any Christian living today. What I mean is that under the influence of rare passions like those of Paul, Augustine, or Teresa, the theory and practice of total love have ever since Christ been continually clarified, transmitted, and propagated. So, as a result of the two thousand years of mystical experience that support us, the contact we can make with the personal center of the universe has gained as much in manifest riches as our possible contact with the world's natural spheres after two thousand years of science. Christianity, I would dare to say, is neither more nor less than a "phylum" of love in nature. Now regarded from this point of view, not only is it not stationary, but it is so much alive that at this very moment we can directly observe it undergoing an extraordinary mutation by raising itself to a steadier consciousness of its universal value. ...

This, as we have already said, is the feeling that the most watchful of believers are already beginning to know. But it is, also as we foreshadowed, the fruit of a development taking place in the whole of human thought. If a Christian can today say to his God that he loves him with his whole body and soul and with the *whole universe,* he is not making a sudden and individual discovery; his act is the *manifestation* of a new and general *state* of the noosphere. In the growing riches of its formulation, love not only totalizes the psychological resources of the world at a given moment, but illumines and resumes all the efforts of the past, the two expected conditions by which we could recognize that it truly represents the higher form sought by human energy.

Whence emerges, lastly, the following suggestion.

At two critical points human energy has already assumed the form in which we know it today: first the appearance of life, whence emerged the biosphere; then emergence of thought which produced the noosphere.

Cannot a further and final metamorphosis have been in progress since the birth of love in Christianity: the coming to consciousness of an "Omega" in the heart of the noosphere — the circles' motion toward their common center: *the appearance of the "Theosphere"?*

— "Human Energy" in HE 153, 156–60

·

The universe fulfilling itself in a synthesis of centers in perfect conformity with the laws of union. God, the Center of centers. In that final vision the Christian dogma culminates. And so exactly, so perfectly does this coincide with the Omega point that doubtless I should never have ventured to envisage the latter or formulate the hypothesis rationally if, in my consciousness as a believer, I had not found not only its speculative model but also its living reality.

Christianity is in the first place real by virtue of the spontaneous amplitude of the movement it has managed to create in humankind. It addresses itself to every human being. And to every class of people. From the start it took its place as one of the most vigorous and fruitful currents the noosphere has ever known. Whether we adhere to it or break off from it, we are surely obliged to admit that its stamp and its enduring influence are apparent in every corner of the earth today.

It is doubtless a quantitative value of life if measured by its radius of action; but it is still more a qualitative value which expresses itself — like all biological progress — by the appearance of a specifically new state of consciousness.

I am thinking here of Christian love.

Christian love is incomprehensible to those who have not experienced it. That the infinite and the intangible can be lovable, or that the human heart can beat with genuine charity for a neighbor, seems impossible to many people I know — in fact almost monstrous. But whether it be founded on an illusion or not, how can we doubt that such a sentiment exists, and even in great intensity? We have only to note crudely the results it produces unceasingly all around us. Is it not a positive fact that thousands of mystics, for twenty centuries, have drawn from its flame a passionate fervor that outstrips by far in brightness and purity the urge and devotion of any human love? Is it not also a fact that, having once experienced it, further thousands of men and women are daily renouncing every other ambition and every other joy save that of abandoning themselves to it and laboring within it more and more completely? Lastly, is it not a fact, as I can warrant, that if the love of God were extinguished in the souls of the faithful, the enormous edifice of rites, of hierarchy, and of doctrines that comprise the Church would instantly revert to the dust from which it rose?

It is a phenomenon of capital importance for the science of

the human being that, over an appreciable region of the earth, a zone of thought has appeared and grown in which a genuine universal love has not only been conceived and preached, but has also been shown to be psychologically possible and opera-tive in practice. It is all the more capital inasmuch as, far from decreasing, the movement seems to wish to gain still greater speed and intensity.

— "The Christian Phenomenon" in PM 294–96

The Heart of Teilhard's Faith Questioned and Reaffirmed

Teilhard de Chardin's spiritual vision emerged in the trenches of the First World War and remained with him all his life. An ardent christocentric mysticism was the source of all his energies, the heart of his great faith and devotion, the firm support for his extraordinary faithfulness. This living faith in the living God immersed in the world and all its labors inspired and sustained him through all the vicissitudes of his life and career. Its dynamic strength motivated him to communicate to others a faith to live by, to see and feel and love the heart of God at the heart of a world with its feverish pulse of movement, change, and becoming.

About a month before his death in April 1955, Teilhard wanted to describe his vision once more. It is summed up in his faith in "the Christic," which is also the title of his last major essay. Some time before, he had written to a friend about "... this extraordinary Christic — I want to live long enough to have time to express it more or less as I now see it taking shape, with an ever-increasing sense of wonder." And in his retreat notes of that time he wrote: "Jesus my God, once again the same prayer, the most ardent, the most humble prayer: Make me end well ... end well — that is, let me have had time and op-

portunity to express my Essential Message, the Essence of my Message." *

This essential message is beautifully expressed in "The Christic," which also includes an honest questioning about the validity and coherence of what Teilhard saw and felt throughout his life. But his understanding of the kind of religion needed in the world of today and tomorrow is reaffirmed in terms of the growing awakening of the spirit and a vision of the ever greater Christ.*

The first passage printed below is chosen from the final section of the essay "The Christic" (1955), which includes searching questions and a strong reaffirmation of Teilhard's faith. The second passage takes us back to the early years of Teilhard's writing when he produced his first essays. It was in them that he first expressed his message about communion with God through communion with the world, a vision of great spiritual power conveyed with much personal sincerity and stirring lyricism. The text is taken from the section on "Communion" in the essay "The Priest" (1918), written shortly after Teilhard had made his solemn vows as a Jesuit. The essay prefigures the later *Mass on the World (1923) with its cosmic offering of the world and all of life to a glorious personal, divine center whose energy and love radiates throughout the universe — the living heart of a living world.*

THE RELIGION OF TOMORROW: AWAKENING OF SPIRIT AND VISION OF CHRIST

Where, among the various currents of modern thought, can we hope to find, if not the fullness at least the germ, of what . . . may be regarded as the religion of tomorrow?

---

*Quoted in the introduction to "The Christic" in HM 80.

In this order of ideas, we immediately meet a fact which it is impossible to reject. It is this: the sort of faith that is needed, in terms of energy, for the correct functioning of a totalized human world has not yet been satisfactorily formulated in any quarter at all....

We must admit that if the neohumanisms of the twentieth century dehumanize us under their uninspired skies, yet on the other hand the still-living forms of theism — starting with the Christian — tend to underhumanize us in the rarified atmosphere of too lofty skies. These religions are still systematically closed to the wide horizons and great winds of cosmogenesis, and can no longer truly be said to feel with the earth — an earth whose internal frictions they can still lubricate like a soothing oil, but whose driving energies they cannot animate as they should.

It is here that the power of the "Christic" bursts into view — in the form in which it has emerged from what we have been saying, engendered by the progressive coming together, in our consciousness, of the cosmic demands of an incarnate Word and the spiritual potentialities of a convergent universe. We have already seen how a strictly governed amalgam is effected, in the divine milieu, between the forces of heaven and the forces of earth.... Indeed, once we cease to isolate Christianity and to oppose it to the moving, once we resolutely connect it up to the world in movement, then, however obsolete it may appear, ... it instantly and completely regains its original power to activate and attract.

And this is because, once that "coupling" has been effected, it is only Christianity, of all the forms of worship born in the course of human history, that can display the astonishing power of energizing to the full, by "amorizing" them, both the powers of growth and life and the powers of diminishment and death, at the heart of, and in the process of, the noogenesis in which we are involved.

As I said before, it is still, and will always be, Christianity:

but a "reborn" Christianity, as assured of victory tomorrow as it was in its infancy — because it alone (through the double power, *at last fully understood,* of its cross and resurrection) is capable of becoming the religion whose specific property it is to provide the driving force in evolution....

How is it, then, that as I look around me, still dazzled by what I have seen, I find that I am almost the only person of my kind, the only one to have *seen?* And so I cannot, when asked, quote a single writer, a single work, that gives a clearly expressed description of the wonderful "diaphany" that has transfigured everything for me?

How, most of all, can it be that "when I come down from the mountain" and in spite of the glorious vision I still retain, I find that I am so little a better man, so little at peace, so incapable of expressing in my actions, and thus adequately communicating to others, the wonderful unity that I feel encompassing me?

Is there, in fact, a universal Christ, is there a divine milieu? Or am I, after all, simply the dupe of a mirage in my own mind?

I often ask myself that question.

Every time, however, that I begin to doubt, three successive waves of evidence rise up from the deep within me to counter that doubt, sweeping away from my mind the mistaken fear that my "Christic" may be no more than an illusion.

First, there is the evidence provided by the *coherence* that this ineffable element (or milieu) introduces into the underlying depths of my mind and heart. As, of course, I know only too well, in spite of the ambitious grandeur of my ideas, I am still, in practice, imperfect to a disturbing degree. For all the claims implicit in its expression, my faith does not produce in me as much real charity, as much calm trust, as the catechism still taught to children produces in the humble worshiper kneeling beside me. Nevertheless I know, too, that this sophisticated faith, of which I make such poor use, is the only faith I can tolerate, the only faith that can satisfy me — and even (of this I am certain) the only faith that can meet the needs of the simple souls, the good folk, of tomorrow.

Next there is the evidence provided by the *contagious power* of a form of charity in which it becomes possible to love God "not only with all one's body and all one's soul" but with the whole universe-in-evolution. It would be impossible for me, as I admitted earlier, to quote a single "authority" (religious or lay) in which I could claim fully to recognize myself, whether in relation to my "cosmic" or my "Christic" vision. On the other hand, I cannot fail to feel around me, if only from the way in which "my ideas" are becoming more widely accepted, the pulsation of countless people who are all — ranging from the borderline of unbelief to the depths of the cloister — thinking and feeling, or at least beginning vaguely to feel, just as I do. It is indeed heartening to know that I am not a lone discoverer, but that I am, quite simply, responding to the vibration that (given a particular condition of Christianity and of the world) is necessarily active in all the souls around me. It is, in consequence, exhilarating to feel that I am not just myself or all alone, that my name is legion, that I am "all men," and that this is true even inasmuch as the single-mindedness of tomorrow can be recognized as throbbing into life in the depths of my being.

Finally, there is the evidence contained in the *superiority* of my vision compared with what I had been taught — even though there is at the same time an *identity* with it. Because of their very function, neither the God who draws us to himself, nor the world whose evolution we share, can afford to be, the former less perfect a being, the latter less powerful a stimulant, than our concepts and needs demand. In either case — unless we are going to accept a positive discord in the very stuff of things — it is in the direction of the fullest that the truth lies. Now, as we saw earlier, it is in the "Christic" that, in the century in which we are living, the divine reaches the summit of adorability, and the evolutionary the extreme limit of activation. This can mean only one thing, that it is in that direction that the human must inevitably incline, there, sooner or later, to find unity.

Once that is understood, I immediately find a perfectly natural explanation for my isolation and apparent idiosyncrasy.

Everywhere on earth, at this moment, in the new spiritual atmosphere created by the appearance of the idea of evolution, there float, in a state of extreme mutual sensitivity, love of God and faith in the world: the two essential components of the ultra-human. These two components are everywhere "in the air"; generally, however, they are not strong enough, *both at the same time*, to combine with one another *in one and the same subject*. In me, it happens by pure chance (temperament, upbringing, background) that the proportion of the one to the other is correct, and the fusion of the two has been effected spontaneously — not as yet with sufficient force to spread explosively — but strong enough nevertheless to make it clear that the process is possible — and that *sooner or later there will be a chain-reaction*.

This is one more proof that truth has to appear only once, in one single mind, for it to be impossible for anything ever to prevent it from spreading universally and setting everything ablaze.   — "The Christic" in HM 97–102

LOVE'S THREEFOLD DREAM:
UNION WITH GOD THROUGH
COMMUNION WITH THE REAL

Just as, when I turn my mind and reason to things that lie outside me, I have no right to dissociate myself from their destiny, so I cannot, in my personal being, escape from the divine, whose dominating power I can see growing ever more supreme wherever I look.

Even had I ever imagined that it was I who held the consecrated bread and gave myself its nourishment, I now see with blinding clarity that it is the bread that takes hold of me and draws me to itself.

That small, seemingly lifeless, host has become for me as vast as the world, as insatiable as a furnace. I am encircled by its power. It seeks to close around me.

An inexhaustible and universal communion is the term of the universal consecration.

I cannot, Lord, evade such massive power: I can only yield to it in blissful surrender.

And first, my God, I entrust myself to the generalized forces of matter, of life, of grace. The ocean of energies that our weakness cannot control: upon which we drift — hardly conscious of our heading, hardly able to change our course — this has now become for me the comforting mantle of your creative action. That part of us which is *in nobis sine nobis* — in me, so large a part that my freedom seems to be lost in it — I can feel warm, animated, charged with the organizing virtue of your body, Jesus.

In everything in me that has subsistence and resonance, in everything that enlarges me from within, that arouses me, attracts me, or wounds me from without, it is you, Lord, who are at work upon me, it is you who mold and spiritualize my formless clay, you that change me into yourself.

To take possession of me, my God, you who are more remote than all and deeper than all, you take to yourself and unite together the immensity of the world and the intimate depths of myself.

I can feel that all the strain and struggle of the universe reaches down into the most hidden places of my being.

But, Lord, I do not passively give way to these blessed passivities: I offer myself to them, actively, and do all I can to promote them....

In order to assist your action in me through all things, I shall do more than make myself receptive and offer myself to the passivities of life. I shall faithfully associate myself with the work you effect in my body and my soul. I shall strive to obey and anticipate your least promptings....

To allay your hunger and quench your thirst, to nourish your body and bring it to its full stature, you need to find in us a substance which will be truly food for you. And this food ready to be transformed into you, this nourishment for your flesh, I will prepare for you by liberating the *spirit* in myself and in everything:

Through an effort (even a purely natural effort) to learn the truth, to live the good, to create the beautiful;

Through cutting away all inferior and evil energies;

Through practicing that charity toward people which alone can gather up the multitude into a single soul....

To promote, in however small a degree, *the awakening of spirit* in the world, is to *offer* to the incarnate *Word* an *increase of reality and consistence:* it is to allow his influence to increase in intensity around us.

And this means but one thing, Lord: that through the whole width and breadth of the real, through all its past and through all that it will become, through all that I undergo and all that I do, through all that I am bound by, through every enterprise, through my whole life's work, I can make my way to you, be one with you, and progress endlessly in that union.

With a fullness no human being has conceived you realized, through your incarnation, love's threefold dream: to be so enveloped in the object of love as to be absorbed in it, endlessly to intensify its presence, and, without ever knowing surfeit, to be lost in it.

I pray that Christ's influence, spiritually substantial, physically mortifying, may ever spread wider among all beings, and that then it may pour down upon me and bring me life.

I pray that this brief and limited contact with the sacramental species may introduce me to a universal and eternal communion with Christ, with his omni-operant will and his boundless mystical body.

Corpus, sanguis Domini nostri Jesu Christi custodiant animam meam in vitam aeternam. Amen.

— "The Priest" in WTW 214–18

The American Teilhard Association, founded in 1967, explores ways in which Teilhard's thought provides a context for reexamining crucial contemporary issues. For further information on the association and its services, please write:

The American Teilhard Association
c/o Iona Spirituality Institute
Iona College, 715 North Street
New Rochelle, NY 10851

Membership Information (subject to change): Regular $25; Husband and Wife $40; Student $15; International $40